44590

D0844583

WITHDRAWN

APR   2005

WORLD OF ANIMALS

2

MAMMALS

LARGE CARNIVORES

Big Cats, Dogs, Bears, Hyenas...

PAT MORRIS, AMY-JANE BEER

GROLIER

The coat of the red fox occurs in three color forms: flame-red (1); silver (2); and the indeterminate cross-fox (3).

Library of Congress Cataloging-in-Publication Data

Morris, Pat.
    Mammals / [Pat Morris, Amy-Jane Beer, Erica Bower].
       p. cm. -- (World of animals)
    Contents: v. 1. Small carnivores -- v. 2. Large carnivores -- v. 3. Sea mammals -- v. 4. Primates -- v. 5. Large herbivores -- v. 6. Ruminant (horned) herbivores -- v. 7. Rodents 1 -- v. 8. Rodents 2 and lagomorphs -- v. 9. Insectivores and bats -- v. 10. Marsupials.
    ISBN 0-7172-5742-8 (set : alk. paper) -- ISBN 0-7172-5743-6 (v.1 : alk. paper) -- ISBN 0-7172-5744-4 (v.2 : alk. paper) -- ISBN 0-7172-5745-2 (v.3 : alk. paper) -- ISBN 0-7172-5746-0 (v.4 : alk. paper) -- ISBN 0-7172-5747-9 (v.5 : alk. paper) -- ISBN 0-7172-5748-7 (v.6 : alk. paper) -- ISBN 0-7172-5749-5 (v.7 : alk. paper) -- ISBN 0-7172-5750-9 (v.8 : alk. paper) -- ISBN 0-7172-5751-7 (v.9 : alk. paper) -- ISBN 0-7172-5752-5 (v.10 : alk. paper)
    1. Mammals--Juvenile literature. [1. Mammals.] I. Beer, Amy-Jane. II. Bower, Erica. III. Title. IV. World of animals (Danbury, Conn.)

QL706.2 .M675 2003
599--dc21

2002073860

Published 2003 by Grolier,
Danbury, CT 06816
A division of Scholastic Library Publishing

This edition published exclusively for the school and library market

Planned and produced by
Andromeda Oxford Limited
11–13 The Vineyard,
Abingdon, Oxon OX14 3PX

www.andromeda.co.uk

Copyright © Andromeda Oxford Limited 2003

Project Director:	Graham Bateman
Editors:	Angela Davies, Penny Mathias
Art Editor and Designer:	Steve McCurdy
Editorial Assistants:	Marian Dreier, Rita Demetriou
Picture Manager:	Claire Turner
Picture Researcher:	Vickie Walters
Production:	Clive Sparling
Researchers:	Dr. Erica Bower, Rachael Brooks, Rachael Murton, Eleanor Thomas

Origination: Unifoto International, South Africa

Printed in China

Set ISBN 0-7172-5742-8

About This Volume

All carnivores live by killing other creatures, and the large carnivores covered in this volume include many of the most exciting, dangerous, and yet attractive of all mammals. They all eat flesh, but do not always kill other animals to get it and may instead use the remains of dead animals. Some, such as pandas, feed mainly on plant material; but the larger species, such as lions and tigers, can even be dangerous to humans. Others, such as the smaller cats, feed mainly on small animals, fish, or even insects. Large carnivores are found on all continents except Antarctica. Many are solitary, but some live in groups and even help each other obtain food. Some are active mainly at night, but others hunt during the day. Several species are now in serious danger of extinction. That is because all large animals are less abundant than smaller ones, and also carnivores must be less numerous than their prey. That combination means that certain species must always have been rare. Their numbers have been further reduced because of the threat they appear to pose to people and domestic animals. Several species have fine furs that fetch high prices, encouraging commercial hunters and illegal poachers. Consequently, many large carnivores now have extensive legal protection and major conservation projects aimed at preventing their extinction. The continued existence of large carnivores is important. If they can be conserved successfully, their presence automatically helps preserve viable populations of their prey and other species.

Contents

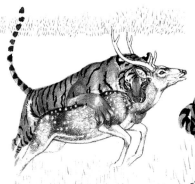

The puma's distribution range stretches the length of America from Canada in the north to Patagonia in the south.

A tiger stalks its prey, then rushes its victim. Usually attacking from the rear, it will aim for the shoulder, neck, or back.

How to Use This Set

World of Animals: Mammals is a 10-volume set that describes in detail mammals from all corners of the earth. Each volume brings together those animals that are most closely related and have similar lifestyles. So all the meat-eating groups (carnivores) are in Volumes 1 and 2, and all the seals, whales, and dolphins (sea mammals) are in Volume 3, and so on. To help you find volumes that interest you, look at pages 6 to 7 (Find the Animal). A brief introduction to each volume is also given on page 2 (About This Volume).

Article Styles

Articles are of three kinds. There are two types of introductory or review article: One introduces large animal groups like orders (such as whales and dolphins). Another introduces smaller groups like families (The Raccoon Family, for example). The articles review the full variety of animals to be found in different groups. The third type of article makes up most of each volume. It concentrates on describing individual animals typical of the group in great detail, such as the tiger. Each article starts with a fact-filled **data panel** to help you gather information at-a-glance. Used together, the three article styles enable you to become familiar with specific animals in the context of their evolutionary history and biological relationships.

Data panel presents basic statistics of each animal

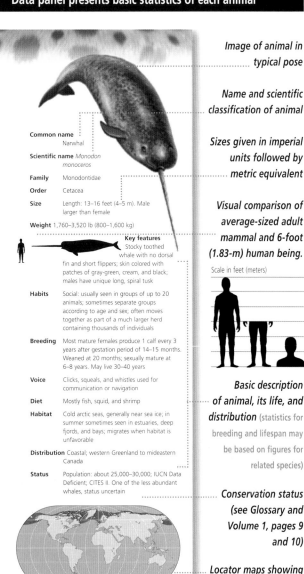

Image of animal in typical pose

Name and scientific classification of animal

Common name
Narwhal

Scientific name *Monodon monoceros*

Family Monodontidae

Order Cetacea

Size Length: 13–16 feet (4–5 m). Male larger than female

Weight 1,760–3,520 lb (800–1,600 kg)

Key features Stocky toothed whale with no dorsal fin and short flippers; skin colored with patches of gray-green, cream, and black; males have unique long, spiral tusk

Habits Social: usually seen in groups of up to 20 animals; sometimes separate groups according to age and sex; often moves together as part of a much larger herd containing thousands of individuals

Breeding Most mature females produce 1 calf every 3 years after gestation period of 14–15 months. Weaned at 20 months; sexually mature at 6–8 years. May live 30–40 years

Voice Clicks, squeals, and whistles used for communication or navigation

Diet Mostly fish, squid, and shrimp

Habitat Cold arctic seas, generally near sea ice; in summer sometimes seen in estuaries, deep fjords, and bays; migrates when habitat is unfavorable

Distribution Coastal; western Greenland to mideastern Canada

Status Population: about 25,000–30,000; IUCN Data Deficient; CITES II. One of the less abundant whales, status uncertain

Sizes given in imperial units followed by metric equivalent

Visual comparison of average-sized adult mammal and 6-foot (1.83-m) human being.

Scale in feet (meters)

	6 (1.83)
	5 (1.5)
	4 (1.2)
	3 (0.9)
	2 (0.6)
	1 (0.3)

Basic description of animal, its life, and distribution (statistics for breeding and lifespan may be based on figures for related species)

Conservation status (see Glossary and Volume 1, pages 9 and 10)

Locator maps showing each animal's normal range

Article describes a particular animal

Scientific name of animal

Common name of animal

Captions to photographs provide additional information about each animal's lifestyle

LARGE CARNIVORES   *Panthera tigris*

Tiger

The tiger, with its black-and-orange striped coat, is one of the most distinctive of all mammals. It is feared the world over, but nowadays the species is severely reduced in numbers.

IN MANY WAYS THE TIGER IS MORE deserving of the title King of Beasts than its close cousin, the lion. It is the largest of all the cats, and its range once extended from the fringes of Europe eastward to Russia's Sea of Okhotsk and south to the Indonesian islands of Java and Bali. Tigers from different parts of this vast range differ considerably, so the species has been divided into eight subspecies. They are named after the region in which they occur, but most can also be distinguished by their appearance. For example, Siberian tigers are consistently bigger than other subspecies, with males weighing up to 660 pounds (300 kg). This almost certainly makes them the biggest cats ever to have lived, including huge extinct species such as the saber-toothed tiger and the cave lion

Common name Tiger

Scientific name *Panthera tigris*

Family Felidae

Order Carnivora

Size Length head/body: 4.6–9 ft (1.4–2.7 m); tail length: 23–43 in (60–110 cm); height at shoulder: 31–43 in (80–110 cm)

Weight Male 200–660 lb (90–300 kg); female 143–364 lb (65–165 kg)

Key features Huge, highly muscular cat with large head and long tail; unmistakable orange coat with dark stripes; underside white

Habits Solitary and highly territorial; active mostly at night; climbs and swims well

Breeding Litters of 1–6 (usually 2 or 3) cubs born at any time of year after gestation period of 95–110 days. Weaned at 3–6 months; females sexually mature at 3–4 years, males at 4–5 years. May live up to 26 years in captivity, rarely more than 10 in the wild

Voice Purrs, grunts, and blood-curdling roars

Diet Mainly large, hooved mammals, including deer, buffalo, antelope, and gaur

Habitat Tropical forests and swamps, grasslands with good vegetation cover and water nearby

Distribution India, Bhutan, Bangladesh, Nepal, China; southeastern Siberia, Myanmar (Burma), Vietnam, Laos, Thailand, and Sumatra

Status Population: 5,000–7,500; IUCN Endangered; CITES I. Previously hunted for fur and body parts, and to protect people and livestock

Different Adaptations
The smallest tigers came from Bali and rarely exceeded 220 pounds (100 kg) in weight. They are now probably extinct. As a general rule, body size relates to the climate and the type of prey available in different parts of the tiger's range. Siberian tigers need to cope with intensely cold and snowy winters, and specialize in catching large prey such as cattle and deer. In contrast, tigers in Indonesia inhabit tropical jungle where overheating is a serious problem for large animals, and the favored prey includes pigs and small deer. The Chinese tiger is thought to be the ancestor of the other types. Fossils show that tigers first appeared in China about 2 million years ago, and they spread north, south, and west from there. Modern Chinese tigers have several traits that zoologists consider rather primitive, including a shortened skull and relatively close-set eyes.

A Bengal tiger wades through water. Tigers are proficient swimmers and can cross rivers that are 4 to 5 miles (7 to 8 km) wide without difficulty.

Juvenile tigers are fond of play fighting, like the one below.

Cross-references to relevant pages in this and other volumes

20 **SEE ALSO** Lion 2:14; Boar, Wild 5:76; Deer and Relatives 6:10

Easy-to-read and comprehensive text

A number of other features help you navigate through the volumes and present you with helpful extra information. At the bottom of many pages are **cross-references** to other articles of interest. They may be to related animals, animals that live in similar places, animals with similar behavior, predators (or prey), and much more. Each volume also contains a **Set Index** to the complete *World of Animals: Mammals*. All animals mentioned in the text are indexed by common and scientific names, and many topics are also covered. A **Glossary** will also help you if there are words used in the text that you do not fully understand. Each volume ends with a list of useful **Further Reading and Websites** that help you take your research further. Finally, under the heading "List of Species" you will find expanded listings of the animals that are covered in each volume.

Introductory article describes family or closely related groups

*A pair of ... prospectors gi... name of "ring... *

Lifesty
Procyo...
gener...
wait...
so to...
ang...
are...
and...

Where Raccoons Live
The procyonids (excluding the red panda) occu...
py a diversity of habitats ranging through most of North,
Central, and South America. The ringtails and cacomistles
are found mainly in rocky cliffs and dry forests, while
coatis prefer more wooded regions. Olingos are found in
American tropical rain forests, while the adaptable raccoons thrive in all of these habitats. The red panda is
confined to Asia, favoring remote, high-altitude forests.
All procyonids are nocturnal, except the coatis, which
mainly active during the day

Detailed maps clarify animal's distribution

At-a-glance boxes cover topics of special interest

Meticulous drawings illustrate a typical selection of group members

Tables summarize classification of groups and give scientific names of animals mentioned in the text

Who's Who tables summarize classification of each major group and give scientific names of animals mentioned in the text

Introductory article describes major groups of animals

Graphic full-color photographs bring text to life

Detailed diagrams illustrate text

Find the Animal

World of Animals: Mammals is the first part of a library that describes all groups of living animals. Each cluster of volumes in *World of Animals* will cover a familiar group of animals—mammals, birds, reptiles and amphibians, fish, and insects and other invertebrates. These groups also represent categories of animals recognized by scientists (see The Animal Kingdom below).

The Animal Kingdom

The living world is divided into five kingdoms, one of which (kingdom Animalia) is the main subject of the

World of Animals. Also included are those members of the kingdom Protista that were once regarded as animals, but now form part of a group that includes all single-cell organisms. Kingdom Animalia is divided into numerous major groups called Phyla, but only one of them (Chordata) contains those animals that have a backbone. Chordates, or vertebrates as they are popularly known, include all the animals familiar to us and those most studied by scientists—mammals, birds, reptiles, amphibians, and fish. In all, there are about 38,000 species of vertebrates, while the Phyla that contain animals without backbones (so-called invertebrates, such as insects, spiders, and so on) include at least 1 million species, probably many more. To find which set of volumes in the *World of Animals* is relevant to you, see the chart Main Groups of Animals (page 7).

Mammals in Particular

World of Animals: Mammals focuses on the most familiar of animals, those most easily recognized as having fur (although this may be absent in many sea mammals like whales and dolphins), and that provide milk for their young.

Mammals are divided into major groups (carnivores, primates, rodents, and marsupials to name just

The chart shows the major groups of mammals in this set arranged in evolutionary relationship (see page 10). The volume in which each group appears is indicated. You can find individual entries by looking at the contents page for each volume or by consulting the set index.

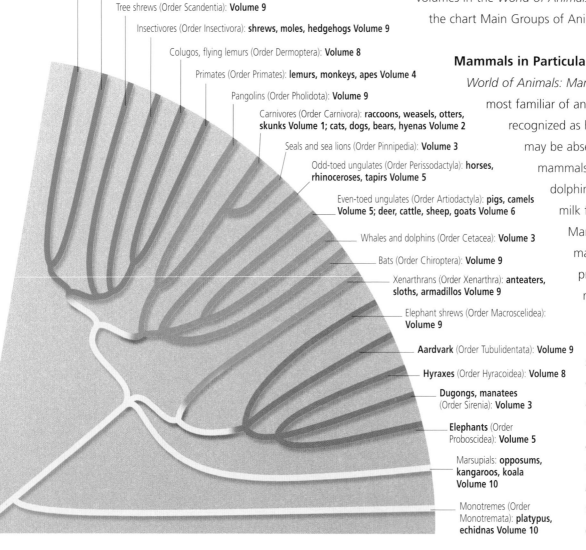

Rodents (Order Rodentia): **squirrels, rats, mice Volume 7; cavies, porcupines, chinchillas Volume 8**

Lagomorphs (Order Lagomorpha): **rabbits, hares, pikas Volume 8**

Tree shrews (Order Scandentia): **Volume 9**

Insectivores (Order Insectivora): **shrews, moles, hedgehogs Volume 9**

Colugos, flying lemurs (Order Dermoptera): **Volume 8**

Primates (Order Primates): **lemurs, monkeys, apes Volume 4**

Pangolins (Order Pholidota): **Volume 9**

Carnivores (Order Carnivora): **raccoons, weasels, otters, skunks Volume 1; cats, dogs, bears, hyenas Volume 2**

Seals and sea lions (Order Pinnipedia): **Volume 3**

Odd-toed ungulates (Order Perissodactyla): **horses, rhinoceroses, tapirs Volume 5**

Even-toed ungulates (Order Artiodactyla): **pigs, camels Volume 5; deer, cattle, sheep, goats Volume 6**

Whales and dolphins (Order Cetacea): **Volume 3**

Bats (Order Chiroptera): **Volume 9**

Xenarthrans (Order Xenarthra): **anteaters, sloths, armadillos Volume 9**

Elephant shrews (Order Macroscelidea): **Volume 9**

Aardvark (Order Tubulidentata): **Volume 9**

Hyraxes (Order Hyracoidea): **Volume 8**

Dugongs, manatees (Order Sirenia): **Volume 3**

Elephants (Order Proboscidea): **Volume 5**

Marsupials: **opossums, kangaroos, koala Volume 10**

Monotremes (Order Monotremata): **platypus, echidnas Volume 10**

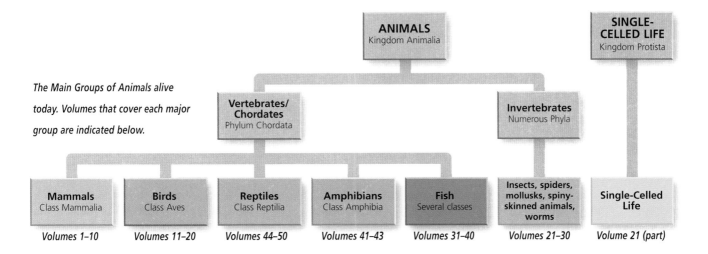

Mammals Class Mammalia	**Birds** Class Aves	**Reptiles** Class Reptilia	**Amphibians** Class Amphibia	**Fish** Several classes	**Insects, spiders, mollusks, spiny-skinned animals, worms**	**Single-Celled Life**
Volumes 1–10	Volumes 11–20	Volumes 44–50	Volumes 41–43	Volumes 31–40	Volumes 21–30	Volume 21 (part)

a few). All the major groups are shown on the chart on page 6. To help you find particular animals, a few familiar ones, such as sheep, goats, cats, and dogs, have been included in the chart.

Naming Mammals

To be able to discuss animals, names are needed for the different kinds. Most people regard tigers as one kind of animal and lions as another. All tigers look more or less alike. They breed together and produce young like themselves. This popular distinction between kinds of animals corresponds closely to the zoologists' distinction between species. All tigers belong to one species and all lions to another. The lion species has different names in different languages (for example, *Löwe* in German, *Simba* in Swahili), and often a single species may have several common names. For example, the North American mountain lion is also known as the cougar, puma, panther, and catamount.

Zoologists find it convenient to have internationally recognized names for species and use a standardized system of two-word Latinized names. The lion is called *Panthera leo* and the tiger *Panthera tigris*. The first word, *Panthera*, is the name of the genus (a group of closely similar species), which includes the lion and the tiger. The second word, *leo* or *tigris*, indicates the particular species within the genus. Scientific names are recognized all over the world. The scientific name is used whatever the language, even where the alphabet is different, as in Chinese or Russian. The convention allows for precision and helps avoid most confusion. However, it is also common for one species to apparently have more than one scientific name. That can be because a particular

species may have been described and named at different times without the zoologists realizing it was one species.

It is often necessary to make statements about larger groups of animals: for example, all the catlike animals or all the mammals. A formal system of classification makes this possible. Domestic cats are similar to lions and tigers, but not as similar as those species are to each other (for example, they do not roar). They are put in a different genus (*Felis*), but *Felis*, *Panthera*, and other catlike animals are grouped together as the family Felidae. The flesh-eating mammals (cats, dogs, hyenas, weasels, and so on), together with a few plant-eaters that are obviously related to them (such as pandas), are grouped in the order Carnivora. These and all the other animals that suckle their young are grouped in the class Mammalia. Finally, the mammals are included, with all other animals that have backbones (fish, amphibians, reptiles, and birds) and some other animals that seem to be related to them, in the Phylum Chordata.

Rank	Scientific name	Common name
Phylum	Chordata	Animals with a backbone
Class	Mammalia	All mammals
Order	Carnivora	Flesh-eaters/carnivores
Family	Felidae	All cats
Genus	*Panthera*	Big cats
Species	*leo*	Lion

The kingdom Animalia is subdivided into phylum, classes, orders, families, genera, and species. Above is the classification of the lion.

LARGE CARNIVORES

The animals in this volume are all members of the group Carnivora. The group includes some of the world's biggest and most exciting predators: the tiger, polar bear, and gray wolf, for example. The following families of mammals have been grouped together in this volume because they are generally larger than other carnivores (meat-eating animals). However, that is not to say that some members of the group are not rather small. The bobcat, for example, is much smaller than the European badger or the giant otter described in Volume 1. But as a close relative of a giant like the tiger, it qualifies here as a large carnivore.

Origins

Fossil records show that many of the largest animals that ever lived are now extinct. During the Miocene and Pleistocene periods (26 to 2 million years ago) there was a general tendency toward the development of giant species, many of which are now legendary—the woolly mammoth or Irish elk, for example. The carnivores were

no exception and once included such formidable beasts as the saber-toothed tiger and the cave bear. However, the largest carnivores that ever lived are still with us—the tiger and polar bear are the largest-ever members of the cat and bear families respectively.

Characteristics

Along with the small carnivores in Volume 1 all these animals have the characteristic carnivore dentition, including long canine teeth and molar teeth with pointed cusps (knobs) on their surface. Four of the largest molars, called the carnassials, are specialized for cutting meat rather than crushing it. However, the larger members of the order Carnivora are less carnivorous than their smaller cousins, and many eat large quantities of plant material. Some, such as the giant panda, are almost exclusively vegetarian. Most bears are omnivores, and many do not have the distinctive carnassials used by meat eaters to cut meat and tough skin.

Among those species that hunt and kill other animals for food, hunting techniques include solitary stalk-and-pounce attacks (most cats), ambush (leopard), wonderful examples of teamwork (lions, African wild dogs), short, fast chases (cheetah), and long, drawn-out pursuits over several miles (wolf). Being large means that many of these animals are able to tackle large prey, and there are few land-dwelling mammals that are not preyed on by at least one large carnivore.

Most large carnivores live solitary lives except when courting and rearing a family, but there are exceptions. In fact, the large carnivores include some of the world's most sociable mammals. Carnivores that live in groups can be models of well-ordered society (such as lions and wolves) or uneasy coalitions of animals drawn together by a clustered food source or the need for security in numbers (brown bears and spotted hyenas, for example).

Most large carnivores are digitigrade, meaning that they have small, neat feet and walk on their toes. Only the bears walk on the whole foot (plantigrade) and appear rather flat-footed and clumsy as a result.

Despite their bulk, large carnivores are often remarkably nimble. Most can run fast, climb well, and several are excellent swimmers. The clouded leopard is acrobatic enough to be able to dangle by one foot from a tree in order to swipe at small prey, and the huge polar bear can sneak across thin ice that would not support a man, using its huge flat feet to disperse the effect of its enormous weight.

Carnivores and Humans

Large carnivores need abundant prey to provide them with enough to eat and must always live well spaced out to avoid consuming all the food available in one place. Therefore they are naturally scarce. That makes them vulnerable when hunting pressures or loss of habitat cause further reductions in numbers. The animals soon become too spaced out to maintain their population, and extinction follows. That is why many larger carnivores are now officially listed as threatened species by the IUCN.

The large carnivores have been traditionally hated by humans because of their predatory habits. Carnivores have been trapped, shot, poisoned, and killed in their dens for centuries. As a result, some are teetering on the brink of extinction, while others have already disappeared. At the other end of the scale two species in particular owe not only their huge success but also their very existence to humans: The domestic dog and cat are the most widespread and numerous large carnivores on earth.

⊖ *A lioness drags the body of a zebra out of reach of scavengers. A large kill is shared amicably by the pride.*

The Cat Family

Cats are perhaps the ultimate carnivores. They are swift runners, agile climbers, and can jump and swim well. Different species specialize in one or two forms of locomotion in order to hunt their preferred prey more efficiently. Cats have short, rounded heads, lithe, muscular bodies, and are deep chested to accommodate large lungs. They also have long legs ending in five toes on the forefeet and four on the back. Except for the cheetah, all cats have very sharp, hooked claws that retract into fleshy sheaths to prevent them from becoming chipped or blunted. The cheetah—the most ancient type of cat alive today—has underdeveloped claws that cannot retract.

What Is a Cat?

In terms of anatomy cats are all very similar: Take away the skin, and it would be difficult to tell most species apart other than by size. This varies considerably from the tiny 13–20 inch (34–50 cm) long, 3.3–6 pound (1.5–2.7 kg) black-footed cat (*Felis nigripes*) to the largest tigers, which can measure 9 feet (2.8 m) long and weigh over 660 pounds (300 kg). The earliest cats appeared about 50 million years ago in the Eocene period. They were initially quite small, but by the Oligocene period (30 million years ago) the family was dominated by huge saber-toothed cats, such as the infamous *Smilodon fatalis*. This awesome animal was the size and weight of a modern lion, with greatly elongated upper canine teeth. It could not bite hard or chew; indeed, the jaws were not particularly strong. All the power came from huge neck muscles, which enabled the cat to open its mouth cavernously wide and use its teeth like daggers (or sabers), slashing and stabbing at the major arteries in the prey's throat.

Saber-toothed cats were the dominant mammalian predators on earth until about 2 million years ago. The last few individuals died out as recently as the last ice age, 10,000 years ago. Saber-toothed cats would certainly have still been around during the Stone Age, when they must have been a terrifying prospect for humans living at the time. Their ancient bones are common in the glutinous traps created by oil seepages, such as those at La Brea in the suburbs of Los Angeles.

Well Balanced

Cats have a famous ability to land on their feet. Even in free fall they can sense which way is up and rapidly twist their heads into an upright position. Most cats have a long tail, which they use to help their balance when running and climbing. Usually the tail is carried in a downward curve, but some cats occasionally hold theirs upright. In many species the tip of the tail is black, which probably helps make it more visible to young when they are following their mother.

Cats have large, forward-facing eyes and good eyesight. A layer of reflective material behind the retina at the back of the eye (called the *tapetum lucidum*) helps direct as much available light as possible onto the retina, improving visual sensitivity and giving cats their excellent

Family Felidae: 4 genera, 37 species	
Acinonyx	1 species, cheetah (*A. jubatus*)
Panthera	5 species, lion (*P. leo*); tiger (*P. tigris*); leopard (*P. pardus*); snow leopard (*P. uncia*); jaguar (*P. onca*)
Felis	30 species, including domestic cat (*F. catus*); bobcat (*F. rufus*); lynx (*F. lynx*); puma (*F. concolor*); ocelot (*F. pardalis*); serval (*F. serval*); wildcat (*F. silvestris*); black-footed cat (*F. nigripes*); caracal (*F. caracal*); tiger cat (*F. tigrinus*); jaguarundi (*F. yaguarondi*); sand cat (*F. margarita*); jungle cat (*F. chaus*); leopard cat (*F. bengalensis*); Asiatic golden cat (*F. temmincki*)
Neofelis	1 species, clouded leopard (*N. nebulosa*)

⊙ *The caracal, a small cat from Africa and the Near East, is distinguished by large, tufted ears and a slender face. Caracals are agile hunters that, like servals, make acrobatic leaps into the air to catch prey.*

 SEE ALSO Lion **2:**14; Tiger **2:**20; Cheetah **2:**26; Leopard **2:**30; Jaguar **2:**36; Puma **2:**42; Ocelot **2:**44; Wildcat **2:**48

night vision. This layer is what makes a cat's eyes appear to glow in the dark when caught by a bright light such as a car headlight. The long-held mystical reputation of cats may be partly explained by their "eyeshine." In fact, the word "lynx" comes from the Greek, meaning "to shine."

Night Stalkers

Most cats are active at night, some exclusively so, and their sensitive whiskers provide a useful backup to vision. The length of the whiskers is related to the size of the cat. If a cat can push its head into a space without its whiskers touching the sides, it can proceed with confidence, knowing that the rest of its body will follow without getting jammed. Cats also have an excellent sense of hearing, and many are able to pinpoint prey using their large ears to focus on small, directional sounds. Compared with dogs, cats do not have a particularly well-developed sense of smell.

Nevertheless, scent is still important as a means of communication, especially among the more territorial species, such as tigers and jaguars. All cats use urine, feces, and scratches to mark out their home patch. In common with several other mammals, cats have an extrasensory organ in the mouth, called Jacobson's organ. Using a sense similar to smell, cats are able to detect chemicals in the air, particularly sex pheromones (a chemical substance produced by an animal in order to stimulate others of the same species).

⊕ Ten species of small cat, shown left to right, reflecting their west (America) to east (Asia) distribution: ocelot (1); tiger cat (2); jaguarundi (3); European wildcat (4); African wildcat (5); black-footed cat (6); sand cat (7); jungle cat (8); leopard cat (9); Asiatic golden cat (10). The range of the cat family is extensive and includes all continents except Antarctica and Australasia.

Domestic Cats

The domestic cat has been honed by centuries of selective breeding into about 30 recognized breeds. While there is fossil evidence of African wildcats living alongside humans as long as 7,000 years ago, it was not until 4,000 years ago that domestic cats became distinguishable from wild ones. Even now the distinction is hazy, since true wild and feral (gone wild) cats interbreed readily.

In ancient Egypt cats were revered as gods. Thousands of mummified cats have been discovered entombed alongside the Pharaohs, and one entire city, known as Bubastis, appears to have been built in their honor by a cult of cat worshippers.

A bronze sculpture of an Egyptian cat dating from the Saite dynasty (about 600 BC).

A Coat of Many Colors

Cats have highly variable coats, including some that are lustrous and spectacularly beautiful. The fur can be short and sleek or deep and fluffy. The background color varies from white to black and includes all shades of gray, buff, yellow, orange, red, and brown. The coat can be plain or marked with spots, blotches, stripes, rosettes, and streaks. Each one is as unique as a fingerprint, so individual cats can often be told apart by their coat patterns. The function of the patterns is usually to break up the cat's outline, making it difficult to see in its favored habitat.

For some cats their superb coat has attracted unwelcome human attention, and many species have a long history of hunting by humans. The fashion for cat fur peaked in the 1960s, when hundreds of thousands of cats, especially big spotted ones, such as leopards, ocelots, and jaguars, were killed for their coats. Some

1 2 3 4 5

pelts could fetch several hundred dollars apiece. Consequently, many species are now rare or extinct in large parts of their former range.

Where Cats Live

The natural range of the cat family is extensive, including all continents except Antarctica and Australasia. Until the introduction of domestic animals all over the world, cats were absent from most islands. Cats occupy all kinds of habitats from dense jungle or coniferous forest to tropical grassland, tundra, deserts, and mountains. Some cats, such as the snow leopard, are highly adapted to a particular niche. Others are true generalists: In fact, the leopard, puma, and wildcat are among the most widespread of all mammals.

Lifestyle

Except for courting pairs and mothers with offspring, most cats are solitary animals. In some species home ranges may overlap extensively, but the occupants are still at pains to avoid each other. Other species are highly territorial, and intruders are met with outright hostility. However, some cats—especially lions—are more tolerant of company and live in prides of related animals.

The size of a cat's home range is less important than the content. Solitary cats, in particular, need a safe den in which to rear their family. A single cat may have several dens or favorite hiding places within its range, and they can include caves, hollow trees, and thickets of dense vegetation. The other vital requirement is an adequate supply of prey. Prey species range from huge wild cattle to the tiniest mouse or even beetles.

Hunting techniques vary surprisingly little, and almost all are based on stalk and dash or sometimes an ambush, followed

⊕ *A pride of lions in the Serengeti National Park, northern Tanzania (Africa). Lions are by far the most social of the cats. The pride is the unit of social life and usually consists of three to 10 adult females, their offspring, and a coalition of two to three adult males. Some prides have been known to contain as many as 18 adult females and 10 adult males.*

by a leap or pounce that knocks the prey over or pins it down. Vertebrate prey is usually killed with a bite to the neck or a stranglehold on the throat. Solitary cats that kill large animals often go to great lengths to hide their half-eaten prey so they can return to feed over several days. For social species, like the lion, teamwork raises the kill rate and allows some adult members of the pride the luxury of not having to catch their own food.

Young cats are born blind and helpless, and rely entirely on their mothers for an extended period. Weaning can begin quite early, but it is months or even years before the kittens can fend for themselves.

6

7

8

9

10

Common name Lion

Scientific name *Panthera leo*

Family Felidae

Order Carnivora

Size Length head/body: 5–8 ft (1.4–2.5 m); tail length: 27.5–41 in (70–105 cm); height at shoulder: 42–48 in (107–123 cm). Male 20–50% bigger than female

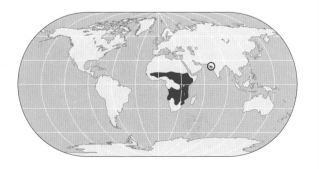

Weight 265–550 lb (120–250 kg)

Key features Huge, muscular cat with long, thin tail tipped with black tuft; body light buff to tawny brown; male develops thick mane of dark fur; head large with powerful, crushing jaws; eyes yellowish-brown

Habits Lives in prides; hunts alone and cooperatively; most active between dusk and dawn; rests up to 21 hours per day

Breeding One to 6 cubs (average 3–4) born after gestation period of 100–119 days. Weaned at 6–7 months; sexually mature at 3–4 years. May live up to 30 years in captivity, rarely more than 13 in the wild

Voice Variety of puffs, grunts, snarls, and roars

Diet Large mammal prey, including antelope, giraffe, zebra, hogs, and buffalo; also carrion

Habitat Savanna grasslands, open woodlands, desert margins, and scrub

Distribution Scattered populations in sub-Saharan Africa; population in Gir Forest, northwestern India

Status Population: several thousand; IUCN Vulnerable; CITES II. Asian lions fewer than 300; IUCN Endangered; CITES I. Declining outside protected areas

Lion

Panthera leo

Lions are by far the most social of the cats, breeding and hunting in large family groups. The male, with his magnificent mane, is much larger than the female, but lionesses are the superior hunters.

THE LION HAS ALWAYS BEEN REGARDED with awe. It is enshrined in the myths and legends of many cultures, and its popular image as the King of Beasts goes back to ancient times.

Widespread

Fossil evidence and cave paintings show that lions were once among the world's most widespread land-dwelling animals, second only to humans. During the Pleistocene era (2 million to 10,000 years ago) there were lions not only in Africa but throughout Eurasia and the Americas. The American and northern European varieties went extinct after the last ice age as forests grew up and human hunters advanced, depleting stocks of the lion's main prey. In southern Europe and the Middle East lions lasted a lot longer. The Greek scholar and philosopher Aristotle wrote about lions in 300 BC, and the Romans made grisly sport of pitting the animals against Christians condemned to death. Such lions were captured in North Africa, but the species is now extinct there. Lions were relatively common in the Middle East 500 years ago, and some survived there until as recently as the early 1900s.

Lions have been killed for a variety of reasons, including sport and self-defense. They are not instinctive man-eaters, but they will resort to attacking livestock and people if the availability of natural prey such as deer or antelope is reduced. Lions can become a serious threat to people involved in farming or other activities that bring humans into lion country. One pair of lions reportedly killed and ate 124 people in Uganda in 1925. The victims were

⬆ *Lionesses and cubs keep a close watch on a resting rhinoceros. A rhinoceros can defend itself with the use of its deadly horns, and the lionesses are cautious of approaching.*

Asian Lions

An Asian lion and lioness. Asian lions belong to a separate subspecies from African lions.

The only wild lions living outside Africa today survive in the Gir Forest, a tiny pocket of protected land in northwestern India. They belong to a distinctive and highly threatened subspecies, *Panthera leo persica*, known as the Asian lion.

Asian lions differ from their African cousins in that the males have a much shorter mane, which does not cover the ears or chest. Both sexes have a fold of skin running lengthwise along the belly.

The decline of the Asian lion was largely a result of persecution by humans. In the days of the British Raj shooting lions was a popular pastime. Marksmen showed their hunting prowess by making hundreds of kills. The population dropped to an all-time low of fewer than 100 animals at the start of the 20th century, by which time the Asian lion had been declared a protected animal.

There are currently 120 or so Asian lions living in captivity around the world. While there may be enough to prevent their extinction, the future of Asian lions in the wild is far from secure. The Gir Forest Reserve is now too small for the 250 or so lions that live there. In times of prey shortage they resort to attacking livestock; some have even become man-eaters. Between 1988 and 1991 Gir lions killed 20 people. It is not surprising that suggestions to release some to other reserves in India have met with stiff opposition.

working on the construction of a new railway, a project that eventually had to be abandoned. Today in Africa humans and lions get along much better because most lions now live in large conservation areas such as the great national parks of Kenya, Tanzania, and southern Africa. Here they have the space and prey they need to survive without attacking people, and they contribute to the local economy by attracting fee-paying tourists.

About 20 percent of African lions are nomadic. They live in small groups, the members of which come and go. They wander over a huge area, following migratory herds of antelope and zebra. Nomadic lions are nonterritorial, and most encounters are nonaggressive. However, most lions live in resident prides, jealously guarding the same territory for generations.

Boundary Patrol

Defense of the territory is usually done by the males, but the whole pride helps define the boundaries by roaring, scent marking with urine, and regular patrolling. The size of a pride's home range varies considerably,

Vocal Communication

Lions have a varied repertoire of vocalizations. The various sounds are distinctive and are usually accompanied by body language that makes their meaning obvious, even to humans. Members of a pride use a gentle huffing sound to greet and reassure each other, while purring communicates contentment (for example, when being groomed). Mewing sounds are used mostly by cubs and vary from short squeaks of excitement to yowls of distress. Growls and snarls are warning sounds, while charging lions often give a gruff coughing sound. A "woofing" grunt signifies surprise and is often followed by a sharp hissing or spitting to show displeasure. The best-known lion vocalization is, of course, the roar. Males start roaring from the age of one year, females slightly later. A full-blown roar can easily be heard up to 5 miles (8 km) away, and the sound is used to define territorial boundaries and to intimidate rivals. Roaring in chorus enhances the bonds between pride members. Most roaring happens at night.

⊕ *The roar of a lion can be heard over distances of up to 5 miles (8 km) and is used to define boundaries and warn off rivals. Lions also roar after devouring a kill.*

depending on the number of animals in the pride and the local abundance of prey. If food is scarce for part of the year, a pride will range over a much larger area. The ranges of neighboring prides may overlap to an extent, but individual lions usually take care to avoid each other. An intruder in the core part of a pride's range will be driven off ferociously.

The need to defend a territory is the main reason why male lions are so much larger than females, up to half as big again in some cases. They need to be big to chase off rivals. Two competing males will size each other up before fighting, and the inferior male will usually back down and go away without a fight. This reduces the risk of these big and well-equipped animals fatally wounding each other. However, there is a definite home advantage; the resident males are more confident and quicker to launch an attack, so they usually win any contest.

The mane is an important factor in male aggression. For a start, a male with a huge mane may be able to fool opponents into believing that he is more powerful than he actually is. If the bluff does not work and a fight ensues, the mane helps protect the vulnerable area around the neck and throat from slashing claws and teeth. The now extinct Barbary lion, a subspecies that lived in North Africa until 1920, had a huge mane that extended well down its back and under its belly.

Female Hunters

The adult male members of a pride do little hunting. Males are capable of catching their own food, but they are rarely as good at it as the females. A large male with a bulky mane will find it difficult to remain inconspicuous, while a slim lioness can creep forward with her body pressed flat to the ground, making use of even very sparse cover. The chances of making

⬇ *A lioness with her cubs. The boisterous rough-and-tumble games of the cubs are tolerated by all members of the pride, since everybody is closely related. Cubs are even allowed to suckle from any female in the group. At less than a year the young cubs will join the lionesses in the hunt, but they are usually more of a hindrance than a help!*

Social Creatures

Lions are by far the most social of the cats. While some individuals live alone, a solitary lifestyle is the exception rather than the rule and loners are usually old males that have been ousted from a pride. Such animals rarely live long.

Lion prides are based on a group of related females, including sisters, daughters, mothers, and grandmothers, most of whom stay with the pride throughout their lives. Females will only be required to leave if the pride gets too big. In such cases small groups splinter off and try to start their own pride. The adult males of the pride are not permanent. In fact, they rarely last more than three or four years before they are displaced by younger, stronger animals. Young males are forced to leave the pride in which they were born at about the time they reach puberty (two to three years of age).

Males often team up to defend a pride. Such coalitions almost always consist of related males (brothers or cousins). On taking over a pride, by killing or driving out the previous males, the first priority is getting the females pregnant. Because female lions cannot breed while they are still suckling young cubs, the males usually kill any cubs younger than about 24 months. Older cubs (especially females approaching breeding age) may escape with their lives, but young males are rarely permitted to remain. The pride females are more inclined to defend older cubs in which they have invested a great deal of care; but on the whole they seem to accept the loss of their cubs and a new boss, and get on with raising a new family.

A receptive female may mate 50 or more times in 24 hours, usually, but not always, with the same male. When the cubs arrive three or four months later, they are usually allowed to suckle from any female, and their boisterous games are tolerated and even encouraged by all members of the pride. This extraordinary benevolence stems from the fact that the members of the pride are closely related. An adult male cannot be sure that the cubs are his offspring, but most will carry his genes and be worth nurturing.

a kill increase when lionesses hunt together. They are highly organized, with different lionesses taking on specialized roles. One female usually takes the lead, selecting the target and signaling the start of the hunt. The fastest females do the chasing, while others ambush and disable the prey. Sometimes the whole pride will join in, fanning out and surrounding the victim. Excitable young cubs are often of little help, but by the age of one year they can make a useful contribution.

Surprise Attack

The lion's hunting technique is all about stealth and surprise. It can run up to 38 miles per hour (60 km/h), but only for short distances. To catch a fleet-footed target such as an impala or zebra, lions need to be within 50 yards (46 m) before launching an attack. They do not usually jump on top of their prey. Instead, they try to knock it off balance with a mighty swipe of the front feet aimed at the prey's flank or rump. Once the prey has been pulled down, the lion clamps its mouth over the throat or muzzle, killing by strangulation or suffocation. The lion can breathe deeply through its nose, so it can keep a tight hold of the prey for as long as necessary, even after a hard chase.

Scavengers

Only about a quarter of hunts are successful, and lions also feed by scavenging. In fact, for some prides four out of five meals are stolen from hyenas, a statistic that contradicts the long-held belief that hyenas routinely harass lions and scavenge their kills. It is actually the opportunist lions that use their superior size and strength to drive the hyenas away.

If the carcass is large, the pride will share the food fairly amicably. On smaller kills there is a definite order of seniority. The males feed first, and young cubs go last. If food is scarce, the cubs are the first to starve.

⊖ *An adult lion needs to eat an average of 11 to 15 pounds (5 to 7 kg) of meat a day. Males get a good share of a kill, even if they have not participated in the hunt.*

Common name Tiger

Scientific name *Panthera tigris*

Family Felidae

Order Carnivora

Size Length head/body: 4.6–9 ft (1.4–2.7 m); tail length: 23–43 in (60–110 cm); height at shoulder: 31–43 in (80–110 cm)

Weight Male 200–660 lb (90–300 kg); female 143–364 lb (65–165 kg)

Key features Huge, highly muscular cat with large head and long tail; unmistakable orange coat with dark stripes; underside white

Habits Solitary and highly territorial; active mostly at night; climbs and swims well

Breeding Litters of 1–6 (usually 2 or 3) cubs born at any time of year after gestation period of 95–110 days. Weaned at 3–6 months; females sexually mature at 3–4 years, males at 4–5 years. May live up to 26 years in captivity, rarely more than 10 in the wild

Voice Purrs, grunts, and blood-curdling roars

Diet Mainly large, hooved mammals, including deer, buffalo, antelope, and gaur

Habitat Tropical forests and swamps; grasslands with good vegetation cover and water nearby

Distribution India, Bhutan, Bangladesh, Nepal; China; southeastern Siberia; Myanmar (Burma), Vietnam, Laos, Thailand, and Sumatra

Status Population: 5,000–7,500; IUCN Endangered; CITES I. Previously hunted for fur and body parts, and to protect people and livestock

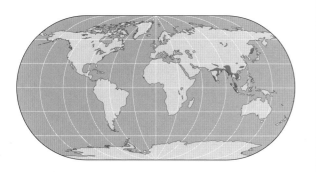

Tiger

Panthera tigris

The tiger, with its black-and-orange striped coat, is one of the most distinctive of all mammals. It is feared the world over, but nowadays the species is severely reduced in numbers.

IN MANY WAYS THE TIGER IS MORE deserving of the title King of Beasts than its close cousin, the lion. It is the largest of all the cats, and its range once extended from the fringes of Europe eastward to Russia's Sea of Okhotsk and south to the Indonesian islands of Java and Bali. Tigers from different parts of this vast range differ considerably, so the species has been divided into eight subspecies. They are named after the region in which they occur, but most can also be distinguished by their appearance. For example, Siberian tigers are consistently bigger than other subspecies, with males weighing up to 660 pounds (300 kg). This almost certainly makes them the biggest cats ever to have lived, including huge extinct species such as the saber-toothed tiger and the cave lion.

Different Adaptations

The smallest tigers came from Bali and rarely exceeded 220 pounds (100 kg) in weight. They are now probably extinct. As a general rule, body size relates to the climate and the type of prey available in different parts of the tiger's range. Siberian tigers need to cope with intensely cold and snowy winters, and specialize in catching large prey such as cattle and deer. In contrast, tigers in Indonesia inhabit tropical jungle where overheating is a serious problem for large animals, and the favored prey includes pigs and small deer. The Chinese tiger is thought to be the ancestor of the other types. Fossils show that tigers first appeared in China about 2 million years ago, and they spread north, south, and west from there. Modern Chinese tigers have several traits that zoologists consider rather primitive, including a shortened skull and relatively close-set eyes.

⊝ A Bengal tiger wades through water. Tigers are proficient swimmers and can cross rivers that are 4 to 5 miles (7 to 8 km) wide without difficulty.

⊙ Juvenile tigers are fond of play fighting, like the two below.

SEE ALSO Lion **2**:14; Boar, Wild **5**:76; Deer and Relatives **6**:10

Subtle differences aside, all tigers have the same adaptations to a predatory way of life. They have long hind limbs that enable them to cover up to 30 feet (10 m) in a single bound. Their forelegs are immensely powerful and armed with long claws that can be retracted when the tiger is walking. The tiger uses this combination to deadly effect when hunting. It usually rushes prey from behind, either knocking it to the ground with the force of its charge or hooking its claws into the rump or flank and dragging the animal over. Smaller prey is dispatched with a bite to the neck. The tiger's canine teeth are long, sharp, and slightly

The Disappearing Tiger

The decline in range and numbers of the magnificent tiger is well documented. Logging and the expansion of agriculture have removed huge areas of tiger habitat. Hunting has also reduced tiger numbers substantially. Of the eight recognized subspecies of tiger the Caspian, Bali, and Javan tigers have become extinct in the last 50 years. Siberian and Chinese tigers are listed by the IUCN as Critically Endangered, and the Sumatran, Indochinese, and Bengal tigers are listed as Endangered.

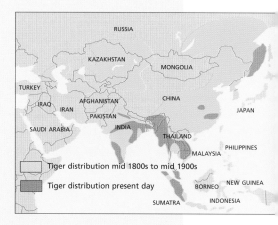

Tiger distribution mid 1800s to mid 1900s

Tiger distribution present day

All tigers are supposed to be protected by international law, but even in some national parks and reserves illegal hunting continues. The biggest threat is the demand for tiger body parts for use in traditional Asian medicine. In the past the main culprits were the Chinese, who have hunted their own wild tigers to virtual extinction. Today tigers are hunted by poachers everywhere. Body parts are then smuggled into China, where they are turned into pills and potions, many of which are exported and sold on the black market for vast sums. Some, such as ground bone to treat rheumatism, can be bought in Asian communities the world over. Demand remains high, despite the lack of scientific evidence that they actually do any good.

Man-Eaters

Tigers are among the few animals known to frequently prey on people. Some tigers even seem to prefer human flesh over that of other species. Sometimes tiger predation has taken a huge toll on human life. For example, over 1,000 people a year were killed in Singapore in the 1940s, 1,000 a year in India in the 1970s, and even now about 100 a year in the Sundarbans mangrove forest near Calcutta. However, these alarming statistics actually relate to comparatively few tigers. Tigers are not born man-eaters; but it seems that once they have made a kill (perhaps after an accidental encounter), some realize the potential of the alternative food source and then exploit it. After all, an unarmed human cannot run fast and is relatively easy to kill. However, most tigers are wary of people and under normal circumstances will avoid any contact. Problem tigers are most common in places where human activity has encroached on their habitat, reducing the availability of natural prey and introducing alternatives such as domestic animals and people themselves.

flattened, and can separate the bones in a victim's spine with ease. A larger animal is more of a challenge; but once it is on the ground, a tiger kills it with a long, suffocating bite around the throat. Even when mortally wounded, a large animal like a gaur could kill a tiger with its flailing hooves, so the tiger maintains the throat bite long after the animal stops struggling, just to be sure it is really dead. It then drags the carcass under some kind of cover before feeding. An adult tiger can eat over 90 pounds (40 kg) of meat in one meal, but with a large kill the tiger is more likely to eat smaller quantities at intervals over the next few days. Sometimes several tigers are seen feeding from one carcass, but they are usually members of the same family.

Necessary Requirements

Although the tiger can live in a variety of habitats, it is restricted to environments that meet three vital requirements: There must be plenty of suitable prey, enough dense cover to allow the tiger to approach prey, and a reliable source of water. Areas of suitable habitat must also be large if they are to support a viable population of tigers. As a general rule tigers live alone, and animals of the same sex tend not to occupy the same range. The size of home ranges varies greatly from place to place, with males in Nepal typically claiming 8 to 40 square miles (20 to 100 sq. km). Male Siberian tigers, on the other hand, may range over 1,600 square miles (4,000 sq. km). Females occupy

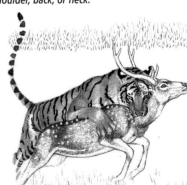

⊕ A tiger needs to attack prey from quite close range. It usually rushes a victim from behind, aiming its claws for the shoulder, back, or neck.

⊕ A leaping Bengal tiger. Tigers have long hind limbs that enable them to leap up to 30 feet (10 m) in a single bound, helping them bring down prey.

much smaller ranges; typically three or four females live within the range of one male, and he can mate with them all.

Tigers tend not to defend territories fiercely, and fights over land are unusual. Nonresident animals seem to respect the owner's rights. Although they may pass through each other's ranges, they do not stay long and keep out of the way. Resident tigers, especially males, visit all parts of their range regularly, leaving scent marks on trees and other landmarks. The marks not only let other tigers know the area is occupied, they also carry information about the individual that made them, such as its sex and reproductive condition. Scent marks fade; and if they are not replaced within three or four weeks, another tiger may attempt to move in. In the case of males this usually means the original resident has died, although females may lose distant parts of their range while they are confined to a small area by the birth of their cubs.

↑ A white Bengal tiger. All white tigers in captivity are descendants of a white male captured in India in 1951.

White Tigers

There is a rare variety of tiger that lacks the pigment which gives other tigers their characteristic orange coat. The dark stripes are still there, but the coat is otherwise creamy-white. Likewise, the tiger's eyes lack brown pigments and are pale blue. Not surprisingly, such animals have always been considered very special, so much so that they have apparently been eliminated from the wild by hunters and collectors. The last record of a wild white tiger was in 1958. Since then, however, many white specimens have been bred in captivity, and there are currently about 40 in zoos around the world.

Fighting is rare among tigers, but those spats that do occur are more often than not between females with cubs and unfamiliar males. Rearing cubs is the sole responsibility of the females, who are ferocious in defense of their young; a spirited attack may be enough to drive even a large male away. When a male takes over a new range, he will often attempt to kill any young cubs in the area. This is so that the females come into breeding condition sooner, and he can begin fathering offspring of his own. Young tigers are vulnerable for a long time: Fewer than half of all cubs live to more than two years of age, and infanticide (killing of young by adults) is by far the most significant cause of death. Once a male is established in an area and can be confident that all cubs are his own, his murderous tendencies subside, and he rarely makes any attempt to approach families.

Playful Cubs

A female tiger will choose a secure den, such as a cave or dense thicket, to give birth. The young stay there for up to two months while their mother leaves them for short periods in order to feed. After that the cubs emerge from the den; but they do not wander far, and their mother still returns at regular intervals to suckle them. Most of their waking lives are spent playing, building up the strength, agility, and coordination they will later use to deadly effect. By the age of five or six months the family begins to accompany their mother to hunt. By 11 months they are capable of catching and killing smaller prey items. Even so, they will still depend on their mother for at least part of their food until they are 18 months old and often remain under her protection for a further year. After that they move on, usually joining the ranks of nonbreeding, largely nomadic tigers that occupy marginal habitats on the fringes of occupied ranges, awaiting an opportunity to claim a range of their own.

⊖ *Licking cubs with the tiger's rough, hairy tongue helps keep them clean. Young tigers leave their mother, or may be pushed out, at the time her next litter is due.*

Common name Cheetah

Scientific name *Acinonyx jubatus*

Family	Felidae
Order	Carnivora
Size	Length head/body: 44–59 in (112–150 cm); tail length: 24–31 in (60–80 cm); height at shoulder: 26–37 in (67–94 cm)
	Weight 46–159 lb (21–72 kg)
Key features	Very slender, long-limbed cat with small head, rounded ears, and long tail held in low sweep; fur pale gold to tawny, paler on belly with black spots; end of tail has dark bands
Habits	Diurnal; can be solitary and nomadic or live in small groups
Breeding	Litters of 1–8 (usually 3–5) cubs born at any time of year after gestation period of 90–95 days. Weaned at 3–6 months; sexually mature at 18 months but rarely breeds before 2 years. May live up to 19 years in captivity, up to 14 in the wild, but usually many fewer
Voice	Purrs, yelps, moans, and snarls; also a high-pitched churring; females use birdlike chirping to reassure young
Diet	Mostly gazelles and impalas; other hoofed animals depending on opportunity
Habitat	Savanna grassland, scrub, and semidesert
Distribution	Widespread but scattered populations throughout sub-Saharan Africa, excluding the Congo Basin. Small population in Iran
Status	Population: fewer than 15,000; IUCN Vulnerable; CITES I. Range and population greatly reduced, now protected in most of its range

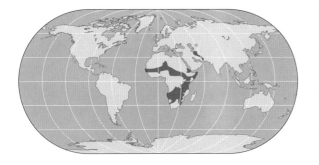

Cheetah

Acinonyx jubatus

Built for speed, the cheetah is the world's fastest land animal. However, its extraordinary sprinting ability is no defense against habitat loss and other pressures that threaten its existence.

THE CHEETAH IS THE FASTEST animal on four legs. Over even ground it can reach speeds of 65 miles per hour (105 km/h), and it has powers of acceleration that rival many modern sports cars. Its body is long and lean, like that of a greyhound, and its spine is remarkably flexible, allowing it to take huge strides that carry it forward up to 26 feet (8 m) in one bound.

Unrivaled Sprinter

The cheetah's legs are long but very slender, the lightness of the bones reducing the need for huge muscles. The paws are small but hard, with blunt, nonretractile claws that help it turn very fast. No other mammal has such extreme adaptations to speed, and none comes close to the cheetah in terms of sprinting ability. The fastest greyhounds, honed by centuries of selective breeding, reach about 40 miles per hour (65 km/h) over short distances. The American pronghorn antelope can run fast for longer distances, but cannot match the cheetah for acceleration and sprints.

The cheetah has made sacrifices for its supreme speed. Compared with other big cats, it has little stamina. In spite of the enlarged lungs and heart that keep oxygen circulating as fast as possible to the cheetah's muscles, it cannot keep up a full pursuit for more than about a minute. Three in every four hunts fail because the cheetah cannot get close enough to the prey before launching an attack.

The cheetah is not particularly powerful, and its relatively small teeth and claws do not make good weapons. The teeth have to be small in order to make room for the enlarged nostrils that enable the animal to breathe efficiently when running and when strangling

⊕ *A cheetah's power of acceleration and sprinting ability are unmatched by any other mammal. However, it begins to tire after 30 seconds and after a minute has virtually no chance of making a kill.*

 SEE ALSO Lion **2:**14; Tiger **2:**20; Leopard **2:**30; Impala **6:**86; Gazelle, Thomson's **6:**94

its prey with a vicelike throat hold. But once the prey is dead, the cheetah has to spend a few minutes getting its breath back before dragging the prey to a secure place as fast as possible. If a scavenger spots the carcass, all the cheetah's efforts may have been for nothing, since it will rarely defend a kill against lions or hyenas. Cheetahs can even be scared off by vultures, although this may have more to do with the fact that vultures attract other, larger scavengers than a fear of the birds themselves.

Wasted Energy

If forced to abandon its hard-earned meal, a cheetah has to chase and kill again, using up yet more energy to feed itself. Being disturbed and driven off its food is a constant threat. Even in national parks where they are safe from other dangers, cheetahs are often forced by tourist buses to abandon their prey to scavengers.

Cheetahs do not seem to target old, young, or sick prey like other large carnivores, nor do they try to approach downwind. They simply select the animal that is nearest them or one that is separate from the main herd and then try to outrun it. Mothers with cubs have a particularly hard time. They need to kill a gazelle or impala almost every day to keep their families well fed (compared with one every two to five days when there are no cubs). Before the age of three months, when they begin to gain some hunting sense of their own, the cubs can be a serious hindrance.

⊕ *An adult cheetah stands among tall savanna grasses in Zimbabwe, southern-central Africa. Scattered cheetah populations are found throughout sub-Saharan Africa.*

A cheetah suffocates a gazelle in Kenya. The animal's enlarged nostrils allow it to breathe efficiently while keeping a vicelike hold on its victim's throat.

Solitary Females

Female cheetahs are generally solitary. Unusually among cats, they have much larger home ranges than males, anything from 20 to 580 square miles (50 to 1,500 sq. km). They cannot hope to defend an area this size, and the ranges of several females usually overlap, although they rarely meet.

Males, on the other hand, are highly territorial, but unlike females rarely live alone. Territories are in such demand that the males have to team up in order to defend one. Such teams are known as coalitions and often contain two or three males, usually brothers. By working together, they can keep other males off their patch and win access to any females that might pass through. Cheetahs are not generally aggressive animals, but males from different coalitions have been known to fight to the death over females and territory. Fights within a coalition are very rare.

A pair of cheetahs may mate several times over a couple of days, but then they go their separate ways. The female gives birth in a secluded spot, usually in dense vegetation. The cubs are blind and helpless at birth, and the mother goes to great lengths to keep them hidden. She will move them one by one to a new hiding place if she suspects they have been spotted. After five weeks, however, they are able to follow her around.

For the first three months young cheetahs have a cape of long gray fur covering the back of the head, the shoulders, and back. It helps disguise their outline in long grass. Despite their camouflage and the mother cheetah's best efforts, the great majority of cheetah cubs do not survive to independence. Estimates of infant and juvenile mortality vary from 70 to 95 percent. A great many are killed by lions and hyenas, while many others starve or succumb to disease or congenital birth defects.

Threatened Existence

Cheetahs need open country with patches of tall grass or other vegetation, which they can use as cover when ambushing prey. However, much of this type of habitat has been given over to agriculture, depriving cheetahs of places to live. Hunting also took a grave toll on cheetah numbers in the past and remains a serious problem in some places.

Cheetah populations have undergone a worrying decline in recent years, despite legal protection for the species almost everywhere. At one time the species was widespread throughout Africa, the Middle East, and

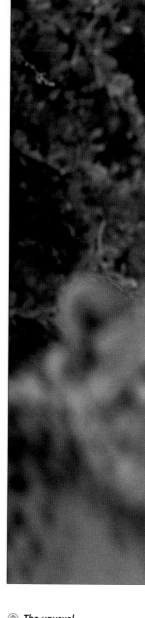

The unusual markings of a king cheetah. The coat pattern is blotchier than that of the majority of cheetahs and is due to a rare gene, like that found in albinos.

A typical family of three cubs. The youngsters will remain with their mother for up to six months before becoming fully independent.

southern Asia. Now there is only one population left outside Africa. It consists of a mere 250 animals and is found in northern Iran. In Africa the cheetah's distribution is now highly fragmented, and the small remaining populations are in danger of becoming inbred.

Studies of cheetah genetics have shown that there is very little individual variation. It seems that at some point in the past the cheetah population must have been extremely small. Today's population is therefore already rather inbred, with all the animals being virtually identical genetically. Now that populations are declining again, there are concerns that their lack of genetic variation could make the whole population vulnerable to disease or other natural disasters to which there will be no inherited resistance.

King Cheetahs

In 1927 zoologists studying cheetahs in Zimbabwe came to the conclusion that there were in fact two species in the area. The second, which they called *Acinonyx rex*, the king cheetah, was distinguished by a much blotchier coat pattern and a "mane" of longer hair around its shoulders. King cheetahs have always been rare, and until recently it was thought that they only occurred in Zimbabwe. However, a wild specimen has since been found on the edge of the Sahara in Burkina Faso, and a number of animals with king cheetah markings have been born in captivity. We now know that king cheetahs are not a separate species or even subspecies of cheetah. They are simply a rare genetic form of *A. jubatus* that turn up in the population, like albinos in other animals. King cheetahs can be born to normal-looking parents and have normal-looking siblings.

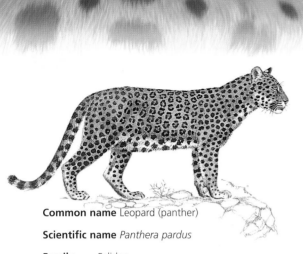

Common name Leopard (panther)

Scientific name *Panthera pardus*

Family	Felidae
Order	Carnivora
Size	Length head/body: 35–75 in (90–190 cm); tail length: 23–43 in (58–110 cm); height at shoulder: 18–31 in (45–78 cm)
	Weight Male 160–200 lb (73–90 kg); female 62–132 lb (28–60 kg)
Key features	Large, lean cat with long tail; pale gold to tawny coat marked all over with black spots arranged into rosettes on back and flanks
Habits	Solitary; mostly nocturnal; excellent climber
Breeding	Litters of 1–6 (usually 2 or 3) young born after gestation period of 90–105 days during favorable season (varies throughout range). Weaned at 3 months; sexually mature at 3 years. May live over 20 years in captivity, probably well over 20 in the wild
Voice	Rasping calls, grunts, and roars
Diet	Mostly small- to medium-sized hoofed mammals; also monkeys, rabbits, rodents, and invertebrates, such as beetles
Habitat	Varied; includes lowland forest, grassland, brush, and semidesert
Distribution	Most of southern Asia and sub-Saharan Africa, excluding rain forests of Congo Basin. Small populations in North Africa, Middle East, Arabia, and China
Status	Population: fewer than 700,000; IUCN Endangered and Critically Endangered (several subspecies); CITES I. Widespread but declining due to habitat loss and hunting

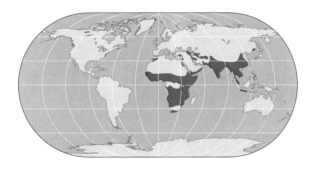

Leopard

Panthera pardus

The leopard is perhaps the archetypal big cat. It can still be found across wide areas of Africa and Asia, but some subspecies are now severely threatened.

THE LEOPARD'S NAME LITERALLY means "lion-panther," with panther or "pard" being the ancient general term for any large cat. Black or "melanistic" leopards, which are common in the forests of Southeast Asia, are still known as black panthers, but so are melanistic jaguars and pumas from the Americas.

Leopards have the largest geographical range of any species of the family Felidae except for the domestic cat. The leopard's range has shrunk over recent centuries, but its decline has not been nearly as precipitous as for other big cats such as the tiger. It still occurs widely in most of sub-Saharan Africa and southern Asia, with a few scattered populations in North Africa and the Middle East. Leopards are more tolerant of people than other large cats and manage to make a living in disrupted habitats that defeat many smaller predators.

Versatile Eating Habits

A large part of the leopard's success is due to its broad diet. It will eat almost any small- to medium-sized animal that it can catch, from an inch-long beetle to a 2,000 pound (900 kg) eland. In southern Africa the diet includes gazelles and impala, in the north wild pigs, in Asia mostly goats and sheep. The leopards in Israel eat rock hyraxes and porcupines, while Arabian leopards eat ibexes, partridges, and the occasional camel. Long-term studies have revealed that at least 90 species are regularly taken as prey, compared with just 12 normally taken by lions. Such versatility means that leopards can live in a wide variety of habitats and avoid direct competition with more specialized predators. Leopards can live almost

⬆ *Leopards are the best climbers of all the big cats and will spend time eating, resting, and sleeping in the branches of a favorite tree. They will even attack prey from tree branches, dropping down onto a victim from above.*

anywhere that provides sufficient cover and food, and they will modify their behavior to take advantage of the most abundant local prey. In some places this means hunting by day instead of night; elsewhere it has caused leopards to attack livestock and even humans.

Tree Dwellers

Of all the big cats, the leopard is the best climber. Its shoulders are especially muscular and provide most of the power necessary to pull it and its prey (often weighing twice as much as the leopard itself) into a tree. Caching (storing) food off the ground keeps it out of reach of most scavengers and gives the leopard the opportunity to feed at leisure. The leopard sleeps and eats in the branches and can descend headfirst, using flexible ankle joints and powerful claws to grip the treetrunk. There will be several favorite trees within a leopard's home range, which the animal returns to time and again. Forest leopards may drop down from the trees onto prey animals passing beneath, but they do not generally lie in wait, and such attacks are opportunistic rather than deliberately planned.

Leopards from different parts of the species' range can be markedly different in size and appearance. The largest individuals live in the well-stocked parks and game reserves of southern Africa, such as Kruger National Park, where males weighing over 200 pounds (90 kg) have been recorded. Elsewhere, leopards are much smaller, with those living in Arabia rarely exceeding 80 pounds (35 kg). Variations in coat color and pattern were used to split the species into dozens of subspecies. Many of them have been reassessed, and there are now about nine officially recognized subspecies based on geographical distinctions as much as on anatomical differences.

⊕ *A common color variation is the melanistic or black leopard. Such animals are often called "black panthers," but so too are black pumas and jaguars.*

During the 1960s over 50,000 leopards were killed every year to satisfy the demand for fashionable fur coats and stoles. Many populations were reduced to critically low levels: The leopard is now listed on Appendix I of CITES, so trade in skins and other parts is restricted and tightly controlled. Killing leopards for sport, however, is still permitted in several African countries where they remain relatively common. Today the demand for skins has been replaced by an increasing demand for body parts for use in traditional Asian medicines, and poaching is a serious problem for some of the more threatened subspecies. The leopard's wide distribution and the varying fortunes of its different subspecies mean that the subspecies are listed separately by the IUCN to draw attention to their status. Separate designations are useful to governments and other organizations trying to incorporate leopard conservation into plans for the development of some of the world's poorer countries, and they help strengthen the case for legal protection.

Home Ranges

Female leopards live in large home ranges, which may overlap at the edges. However, within the range there is always a core area that remains private. Such an area will have a reliable source of prey. It will also contain several trees or other secure places that are suitable for feeding, resting, and for hiding young. Male ranges are significantly larger. They overlap with those of up to six females to whom the male may have exclusive access for breeding. In spite of such a complex mosaic of leopard activity areas, the core of an individual leopard's home is usually respected, and strangers tend to keep away. Overlying male and female home ranges, there may be a third layer of less well-defined ranges occupied by younger, nonbreeding animals. Copious scent marking and vocalizations mean that unrelated leopards hardly ever meet.

Pregnant females do not build a nest, but will give birth to their cubs in a secure part of their core range. They may use a rocky crevice

Vulnerable to Attack

Unlike other members of the genus *Panthera*, which have no natural enemies other than humans, the leopard is vulnerable to attack and harassment by other predators. Young leopards are frequently killed by lions, hyenas, and wild dogs, and even fully mature adults will avoid confrontation with these species. Leopards have been known to abandon freshly killed prey when challenged by a single jackal or domestic terrier—animals less than half their size, which under other circumstances they might easily kill and eat. Females with young to feed and defend are more likely to stand their ground, but on the whole the leopard is strangely reluctant to fight or engage in a standoff that might attract yet more unwanted attention. Apparently, it is simply easier for the leopard to give up its prize and begin hunting again elsewhere.

⬅ A snarling leopard. Despite its ferocious appearance it seems that the leopard is vulnerable to attack by other large predators. It will often choose to give up its prey rather than engage in confrontation.

⬇ A leopard with her cub of three months. Male cubs generally remain with their mother for 18 months, until they learn to hunt successfully. Daughters stay for longer, usually until the mother breeds again.

or ledge as a den, or perhaps a tree hole or thicket of dense vegetation. High branches that make good resting places for an adult leopard would be much too dangerous for the cubs, which are born blind and barely able to crawl. Young leopards spend a long time with their mother. Unless the babies die very young, it will be at least two years before the female breeds again. Young males disperse first and go farthest away, so reducing the risk of inbreeding later on. Their mother will become less tolerant of them as soon as they learn to hunt successfully, usually at about 18 months. Daughters may stay close to their mother much longer and continue to share kills until the next family arrives. After that the younger females have little or no contact with their mother, although they may set up home nearby.

Common name Snow leopard (ounce)

Scientific name *Panthera uncia* (*Uncia uncia*)

Family Felidae

Order Carnivora

Size Length head/body: 39–51 in (100–130 cm); tail length: 31–39 in (80–100 cm); height at shoulder: 24 in (60 cm)

Weight Male 100–121 lb (45–55 kg); female 77–88 lb (35–40 kg)

Key features Long-bodied cat with relatively short legs, small head, and long tail; fur is thick and pale gray to creamy-white, with gray spots and rosettes all over body, except the underside

Habits Active dusk to dawn; solitary; very agile

Breeding Litters of 1–5 (usually 2 or 3) cubs born April–June after gestation period of 90–103 days. Weaned at 2–3 months; sexually mature at 2 years. May live up to 15 years in captivity, 21 in the wild

Voice Soft growls, grunts, and huffing sounds; moans loudly in courtship; does not roar

Diet Mountain animals, including goats, deer, pikas, and marmots; some domestic animals

Habitat Rocky mountainsides and grassy alpine plateaus at 9,000–20,000 ft (2,700–6,000 m)

Distribution Mountainous parts of China, Nepal, Bhutan, India, Pakistan, Afghanistan, Uzbekistan, Tajikistan, Kazakhstan, Russia, and Mongolia

Status Population: fewer than 7,000; IUCN Endangered; CITES I. In decline as a result of hunting; also persecuted by livestock farmers

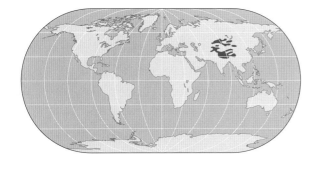

Snow Leopard

Panthera uncia

A large leopard of the high mountains, the snow leopard is a unique species. Although still widely distributed, it is now becoming scarce.

THE RARE AND BEAUTIFUL SNOW LEOPARD is usually classified in the genus *Panthera* alongside big cats like lions and leopards. But in many ways it also resembles small cats of the genus *Felis*, such as the lynx and puma. Unlike other big cats, the snow leopard cannot roar, and its characteristic postures and feeding technique are more like those of the smaller cats. For this reason some zoologists place the species in a genus of its own, called *Uncia*.

Thickly Furred Coat

Whatever its exact relationship with other members of the cat family, the snow leopard is undoubtedly one of the most attractive and enigmatic of all mammals. Its much coveted coat grows up to 3 inches (8 cm) thick and has a dense, woolly underlayer to protect the leopard from the bitterly cold weather in its mountain home. The fur even covers the soles of its huge feet, providing insulation against the icy ground and protection from sharp rocks. It also helps spread the cat's weight so that it can move over the surface of soft snow without sinking in. For an animal that spends most of its life above the snow line, it might be thought that a pure-white coat like a polar bear's would provide the best camouflage. But on the mountainsides of the Himalayas and Hindu Kush there are nearly always exposed gray rocks and stones, and against this type of background a snow leopard's highly patterned coat is virtually invisible.

The snow leopard has other adaptations to the cold, including large nostrils in which air is warmed as it is inhaled and cooled again on the way out. Exhaling warm breath into cold air

 SEE ALSO Leopard **2**:30; Fox, Arctic **2**:70; Bear, Polar **2**:84; Pika Family, The **8**:94

wastes energy; it also creates puffs of condensation that could alert a prey animal to the leopard's presence, and it also could turn to ice on the cat's face. The fur on the face and head is not as thick as elsewhere; so when the snow leopard is sleeping, it curls its tail around as a muffler to keep its nose warm. The tail is extremely long and serves as a counterbalance when the leopard leaps from rock to rock.

Agile Hunter

Despite the chunky appearance created by the snow leopard's thick fur, it is one of the most agile members of the cat family. It is able to leap a vertical distance of about 20 feet (6 m) and is said to be able to travel 50 feet (15 m) in a single bound! This great leaping prowess is an important part of the leopard's hunting technique. So long as it can get close enough to prey like the Himalayan blue sheep, it can bring the animal to the ground and inflict a killing bite in one powerful movement. Large prey are eaten in several sittings over a period of a few days, after which the leopard moves on to a new hunting ground within its range.

Snow leopards occupy overlapping home ranges, but they are generally solitary. The size of the range depends on the local abundance of prey. In Nepal, for example, a leopard may spend most of its life in an area of little more than 5 square miles (12 sq. km). In Mongolia, on the other hand, a range may extend to over 400 square miles (1,000 sq. km) and include large expanses of desert plateau in between mountains.

Snow leopards are suffering greatly from loss of habitat to grazing livestock, and they are often persecuted as pests. Not surprisingly, their fur is highly sought after and even today can be found on open sale in some parts of Asia, despite legal protection. There are probably no more than 7,000 snow leopards left in the wild, and an intensive program of education and law enforcement is required throughout its range if the species is to survive.

⊕ Living on "the roof of the world," the rare and beautiful snow leopard has attained almost mythical status. Its wailing mating cries could be mistaken for those of a yeti.

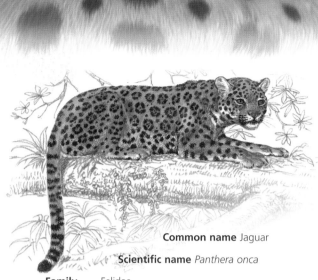

Common name Jaguar

Scientific name *Panthera onca*

Family	Felidae
Order	Carnivora
Size	Length head/body: 44–73 in (112–185 cm); tail length: 18–30 in (45–75 cm); height at shoulder: 27–30 in (68–76 cm)
	Weight Male 200–264 lb (90–120 kg); female 130–200 lb (60–90 kg)
Key features	Large, robust-looking cat with short, thick tail and broad, heavy-looking head; fur pale gold to reddish-brown with spots arranged in rosettes and rings; black individuals known
Habits	Solitary; territorial; active at any time of day but mostly around dawn and dusk; excellent swimmer and climber
Breeding	Litters of 1–4 cubs born at any time of year in tropics after gestation period of 93–105 days (seasonal in north and south). Weaned at 5–6 months; sexually mature at 2–4 years. May live up to 22 years in captivity, 24 in the wild
Voice	Grunts and mews
Diet	Mostly peccaries and capybaras; also tapirs and other mammals; crocodiles and fish
Habitat	Forests, scrub, grasslands, and semidesert; prefers habitats with water nearby
Distribution	Central and South America south to northern Argentina and Paraguay
Status	Population: unknown, probably several thousand; IUCN Lower Risk: near threatened; CITES I. Declining in range and population

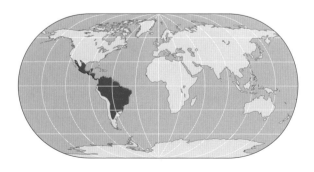

Jaguar

Panthera onca

The jaguar is the Western Hemisphere equivalent of the leopard, occurring widely in Central and southern America.

THE JAGUAR HAS A DISTINCTLY stocky build and short tail compared with its cousin the leopard. It is the largest cat in the Americas, having survived the mass extinction of other large mammals at the end of the Pleistocene era (2 million years ago). It managed to survive by preying on fish and large reptiles, such as crocodiles and turtles, and its massive jaws may have evolved as an adaptation for cracking open turtle and tortoise shells. This explains the jaguar's enduring fondness for waterside habitats; even though much of its prey is nowadays caught on dry land, it still kills by piercing the skull rather than by breaking the neck or strangulation the way other cats normally do.

From Hunter to Hunted

The arrival of European settlers and their livestock in the region probably provided an unexpected boost to the jaguar population in the form of several new species of potential prey. There is evidence that the new feeding opportunities actually increased jaguar numbers for a time. However, this period of growth was short-lived, since people began to hunt jaguars for skins and to protect themselves and their animals from attack. The trade in jaguar skins peaked during the 1960s, when tens of thousands of pelts were exported to Europe and the United States each year. Jaguars rarely attack people, but they will follow unwanted intruders, giving frightened humans the impression they are being stalked.

The range of the jaguar used to extend well into the southern United States, and the animal was once the dominant predator from Florida to Arizona. The last jaguars resident in the United States were probably eliminated quite early in the 20th century. However, wandering animals still occasionally cross the border from Mexico,

⬆ *Jaguars survived extinction 2 million years ago by preying on fish and reptiles. Today they catch most of their prey on land, but still prefer waterside habitats.*

 SEE ALSO Tiger **2**:20; Leopard **2**:30; Tapir, Brazilian **5**:64; Peccary, Collared **5**:90

and in 1996 there were two confirmed sightings in Arizona. But the Mexican population is declining, too, and may number fewer than 500 animals. Elsewhere, the jaguar is doing better, especially now that international law prohibits trade in its skins.

Territorial

Jaguars are territorial, but part of their home range can overlap with that of another individual. Male home ranges are at least twice as large as those occupied by females—up to 160 square miles (about 400 sq. km). Like tigers, male jaguars hold territories by prior right, thereby avoiding the need to fight over land. As long as the male continues to mark out his range, its boundaries will be respected by other males in the area.

Both sexes occasionally leave their range and wander widely, in many cases settling somewhere new. Such journeys may be associated with the movements of prey. Females that wander usually do so when they are ready to breed and may mate with several males along the way. It may be the only way a female can influence which male fathers her offspring, since an adult male can occupy the same range throughout his reproductive life.

⊕ *Entirely black jaguars are relatively common. They are not a different species, but simply a genetically determined color variant.*

Common name Bobcat

Scientific name *Felis rufus*

Family	Felidae
Order	Carnivora
Size	Length head/body: 25.5–41 in (65–105 cm); tail length: 4–7.5 in (11–19 cm); height at shoulder: 17.5–23 in (45–58 cm)
Weight	9–33 lb (4–15 kg)
Key features	Small, slender-limbed, short-tailed cat; fur thick, varies in color from buff to brown with darker spots and streaks; ears pointed, often with tufts; ruff of fur around jowls
Habits	Solitary; territorial; active day or night
Breeding	Litters of 1–6 kittens born after gestation period of 60–70 days, usually in spring. Weaned at 2 months; females sexually mature at 1 year, males at 2 years. May live up to 32 years in captivity, probably no more than 13 in the wild
Voice	Usually silent, but hisses and shrieks in distress and during courtship
Diet	Small mammals and birds; sometimes larger prey, such as small deer; domestic animals
Habitat	Varied; includes forests, scrub, swamp, mountains, and the edges of deserts

Distribution North America

Status	Population: 700,000–1 million; CITES II. Declined in the past due to persecution; still harvested for fur under license in some states

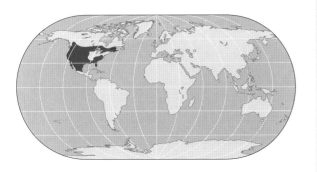

Bobcat

Felis rufus

Territorial and solitary, the bobcat is sometimes confused with its close cousin, the lynx. Both cats have tufted ears and short tails, but the bobcat tends to be the more aggressive of the two.

THE BOBCAT IS SO CALLED because of its short tail, which resembles the docked bobtails of some domestic mammals. It looks a lot like another North American cat, the lynx, but there are few places where the two species live alongside each other. Bobcats are more aggressive than lynx and usually drive the latter out of habitats that suit both. However, the lynx is much better adapted to snow than the bobcat, which has small feet that sink in easily. So the northern limit of the bobcat's distribution is determined largely by the average snowfall.

Adaptable Cats

Bobcats are true generalists, which means they can live in almost any habitat; hence their wide natural distribution throughout most of North America. They are only absent where large areas are intensively cultivated or given over to industrial development. They are scarce in places where they have been overhunted. Their varied diet is a major factor in their adaptability. Their preferred prey appears to be rabbits and hares, but they will eat other small mammals and many larger ones too, including beavers, peccaries, and deer. Hoofed mammals are the main winter prey of bobcats in the north of their range, and Canadian bobcats are usually larger than those living in the south. This helps them cope with bigger prey.

The bobcat's hunting technique almost always relies on surprise. With its mottled coat providing admirable camouflage, a bobcat can sneak up on the most alert of victims, using a combination of stealth and endless patience. The kill is made with a sudden leap and a quick bite to the back of the neck, separating the backbones and severing the spinal cord.

 SEE ALSO Lynx **2:**40; Ocelot **2:**44; Beaver, American **7:**30; Hare, Snowshoe **8:**74

Bobcats can be active at any time of day, but most animals adjust their activity to match that of their preferred prey. They wander up to 9 miles (15 km) a day in search of food, stopping often to mark and re-mark the boundaries of their home range. Females have smaller ranges than males—0.4 to 8 square miles (1 to 20 sq. km)—but they do not overlap with any others. Male territories can be anything from 2 to 16 square miles (5 to 40 sq. km), and they can overlap the ranges of other males and several females.

Respecter of Boundaries

Outside the breeding season bobcats go out of their way to avoid meeting, which leads to intensive scent marking to warn others away. Marks are made with urine and feces, and with secretions from the cat's anal glands. The marking is very effective, and bobcats appear to respect each other's territorial boundaries. Aggressive encounters seem very rare, and the ownership of a particular range area only changes when the resident animal dies.

⊕ *Bobcats are solitary animals. Outside the breeding season they will go out of their way to avoid meeting and seem to respect each other's territories.*

Of course, the need to breed means that males and females must meet at some point, and mating occurs any time between November and August. Most kittens are born in spring, but some births happen much later in the year. If a female loses her first litter of the year when the kittens are very young, she comes into season again and may produce a replacement litter in late summer. The kittens are able to follow their mother after three or four months, and they learn hunting skills by watching her. They stay with her until she is ready to breed again, then head off to find a place of their own.

There are probably about 1 million bobcats living in North America. They are protected in some states, notably those where the species has become rare. Elsewhere, they are hunted and trapped for part of the year, and their pelts sold to the fashion industry.

Common name Lynx (Eurasian lynx)

Scientific name *Felis (Lynx) lynx*

Family	Felidae
Order	Carnivora
Size	Length head/body: 31–51 in (80–130 cm); tail length: 4–10 in (10–25 cm); height at shoulder: 23.5–29.5 in (60–75 cm)
	Weight 18–84 lb (8–38 kg)
Key features	Stocky cat with longish legs and large, furry feet; color varies from pale gray through yellow to reddish-brown; ears tufted
Habits	Solitary; nocturnal; wanders widely
Breeding	Litters of 1–4 kittens born April–June after gestation period of 67–74 days. Weaned at 3 months; females sexually mature at 9–21 months, males at 21–31 months. Lives up to 24 years in captivity, 17 in the wild
Voice	Hisses and mews, but usually silent
Diet	Mostly eats small- and medium-sized mammals, including hares and small deer
Habitat	Mixed and taiga forest, scrub, steppe, rocky alpine slopes
Distribution	Eurasian lynx: northeastern Europe, Balkans, Turkey, and the Middle East excluding Arabia, much of former U.S.S.R., Mongolia, and northern China. Iberian lynx: Spain, Portugal. Canadian lynx: Canada, Alaska, northern U.S.
Status	Population: unknown, but certainly many thousands; IUCN Endangered (Iberian), Vulnerable (Canadian); CITES I (Iberian), II (Canadian and Eurasian). All have declined, mainly as a result of hunting for fur

Lynx

Felis lynx

A stocky, medium-sized cat, the lynx is widely distributed throughout the Northern Hemisphere. It is sometimes considered to be three separate species.

THERE IS AN ONGOING SCIENTIFIC debate about whether the three recognized types of lynx are all members of the same species or not. The Canadian lynx *(F. canadensis)*, Iberian lynx *(F. pardinus)*, and Eurasian lynx *(F. lynx)* look remarkably similar, but they have different behavioral adaptations to suit life in their different parts of the world.

Distinctive Tail

Lynx are close cousins of bobcats, but can be told apart by examining the tail. Both species have short tails, but that of the lynx is completely black at the tip. In contrast, the bobcat's tail tip is black just on top. The largest lynx are Eurasian specimens from Siberia. They live on Arctic hares and other mammals several times bigger than themselves, such as reindeer (caribou). Snow can be an advantage to a hunting lynx, since deer can become bogged down and are then easier to catch. The lynx's feet are large and furry, so its weight is spread over a larger area, allowing it to run across snow without sinking. Iberian and Canadian lynx are about half the size of Eurasian lynx and generally hunt smaller prey.

Feeding Habits

The Canadian lynx feeds almost exclusively on snowshoe hares, and its numbers fluctuate from year to year according to the availability of the hares. Iberian lynx mainly feed on mammals such as rabbits, although they are also able to catch birds and fish, hooking them out of the air or water with a swipe of their sharp claws. For the smaller lynx a rabbit a day is sufficient food, but larger lynx eat rather more. Having killed a big animal such as a deer, they will drag it to safety, eat what they can, and cache (store)

⊕ Snowy conditions can be advantageous for the hunting lynx, since its large, furry feet help spread its weight evenly and stop it from sinking into fresh snow. Lynx will often hunt deer that get bogged down in the snow and so are relatively easy to catch.

SEE ALSO Bobcat **2**:38; Reindeer/Caribou **6**:20; Rabbit, European **8**:68; Hare, Snowshoe **8**:74

the rest for later. Hunting is almost always a solitary activity, although mothers have sometimes been seen helping their fully grown young to hunt. Newly independent lynx sometimes team up with a sibling for the first few months after leaving their mother's care.

Endangered Species

Female lynx mature faster than males and can be capable of breeding within their first year. However, few do so because breeding is regulated by habitat availability. Lynx do not breed until they have found a suitable home range in which it will be possible to rear young. In places like Spain, where habitat is greatly restricted, adult lynx may never get the opportunity to breed. Of the few hundred Iberian lynx left in the wild fewer than a third are thought to be breeding females, making this one of the world's most endangered cats. Canadian and Eurasian lynx are faring better, although both have been extensively hunted in the past. Lynx fur is dense and luxurious, and several thousand animals are still legally shot or trapped every year for their fur.

In Central Europe lynx have been reintroduced to parts of Germany, Slovenia, and Switzerland; and while it is still early days for these cats, there are encouraging signs. The Swiss animals have bred successfully for several seasons, and some have now spread over the Alps into northern Italy of their own accord.

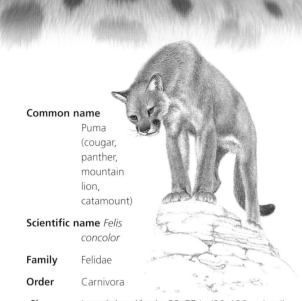

Common name
Puma (cougar, panther, mountain lion, catamount)

Scientific name *Felis concolor*

Family Felidae

Order Carnivora

Size Length head/body: 38–77 in (96–196 cm); tail length: 21–32 in (53–82 cm); height at shoulder: 24–27.5 in (60–70 cm)

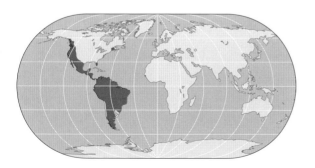

Weight Male 148–264 lb (67–120 kg); female 80–132 lb (36–60 kg)

Key features Large, muscular cat with long legs and tail; small head with large, rounded ears; coat color varies from silvery gray through warm buffy tones to dark tawny

Habits Solitary; active at any time of day; climbs extremely well

Breeding Litters of 1–6 (usually 3 or 4) kittens born January–June after gestation period of 90–96 days. Weaned at 3 months; sexually mature at 2.5–3 years. May live up to 21 years in captivity, rarely more than 14 in the wild

Voice Hisses, growls, whistles, and screams

Diet Carnivorous; mostly deer; also other hoofed animals, rodents, and hares

Habitat Very varied; lowland and mountain forests, swamps, grassland, and scrub

Distribution Most of North and South America

Status Population: many thousands in total, but Florida panther (*F. c. coryi*) fewer than 50; IUCN Critically Endangered (2 subspecies); CITES II (at least 2 subspecies). Persecuted as a pest in the past; now protected in parts of its range although still hunted in other areas

Puma

Felis concolor

The puma is the second largest cat in the Americas and by far the most widespread, with a natural range extending from Canada to Patagonia.

PUMA, COUGAR, PANTHER, AND MOUNTAIN lion are widely used names for the same animal—a highly adaptable, agile predator that feeds on medium-sized prey such as deer. Despite their larger size, pumas are more closely related to lynx and bobcats than to lions and jaguars, and are first cousins to the domestic cat. They are extremely agile and can climb with great ease. They prey mostly on ground-dwelling animals, but often use trees to lie in wait for passing animals, dropping on them from above. Alternatively, they may chase a prey animal for a short distance before leaping on its back. In either case the prey is killed with a bite to the neck. A lone adult puma may only need to kill every two weeks. It will drag the carcass to a safe place and hide it under a heap of dirt and debris, returning to feed on it again and again. For a mother puma with cubs life is rather more demanding, and she may have to kill a deer every three or four days to sustain her family.

Solitary Existence
Pumas are generally solitary, although young cats may stay with their mother for over a year and then remain together a few more months after she has left them. After the family disperses, young pumas live as nomads for a while, wandering through the ranges of resident pumas until they find a place to settle. While they may be capable of breeding by the age of two years, they will not do so until they have established themselves in a suitable home.

Females occupy large home ranges, which may overlap more or less completely with those of other pumas, but they avoid meeting by the use of scent marks and various vocalizations. Except when they have young kittens, females wander widely over their entire range, using

⊙ Pumas have a reputation for killing livestock such as sheep and cattle. In fact, they more frequently kill deer and tend to select old or weak individuals. In so doing they may be helping maintain a healthy deer population.

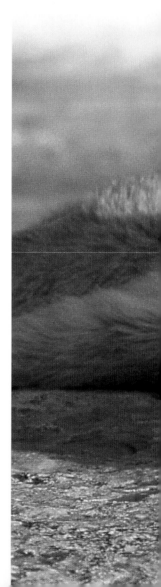

various patches of dense vegetation or small caves to rest in, rather than a regular den. Males operate in a similar way, except their ranges are much larger—sometimes over 400 square miles (1,000 sq. km)—and they overlap only with female pumas, not other males. They use scent marking more frequently than females, especially around the borders of their range. They do not generally fight over territory, and new residents only move in when the previous occupant dies.

Pumas have a reputation for killing livestock such as horses, cattle, and sheep, but that is relatively infrequent. They kill deer, too, but in so doing may actually help keep the deer population healthy, since they tend to select old or weak individuals. It also prevents the deer from getting too numerous. Pumas have been implicated in a number of fatal attacks on humans, but in general they avoid people.

Gradual Comeback

Intensive eradication attempts all but exterminated pumas from much of North America, leaving only small populations in the western mountains, southern Texas, and Florida. The animals appear to be making a gradual comeback in some Midwestern and eastern states, but they are still hunted in Texas. The Florida population is thought to number no more than 50 individuals, despite millions of dollars being spent on their conservation.

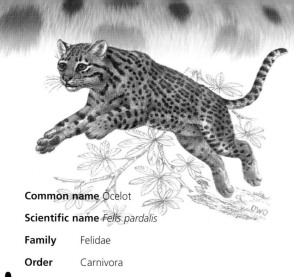

Common name Ocelot

Scientific name *Felis pardalis*

Family   Felidae

Order   Carnivora

Size   Length head/body: 22–39 in (55–100 cm); tail length: 12–18 in (30–45 cm); height at shoulder: up to 20 in (50 cm)

Weight 25–35 lb (11.5–16 kg)

Key features Pale gray to reddish or tawny cat, with variable pattern of dark spots and streaks around blotches of intermediate color; usually has dark tail rings and 2 cheek stripes

Habits   Solitary; nocturnal; can climb and swim well but spends most of time on the ground

Breeding   Litters of 1–3 kittens born at any time of year after gestation period of 79–85 days. Weaned at 6 weeks; females sexually mature at 18–22 months, males at 30 months. May live up to 21 years in captivity, 15 in the wild

Voice   Yowls and meows like domestic cat

Diet   Mainly rodents and rabbits, but known to catch small deer, monkeys, and wild pigs; also birds, reptiles, amphibians, and fish

Habitat   Varied; includes tropical forest, swamp, mountainous areas, and dry scrub

Distribution Southwestern Texas, Central and South America down to northern Argentina

Status   Population: 1.5–3 million; IUCN Endangered (Texas subspecies); CITES I. Possibly recovering in places, but Texas subspecies may number fewer than 100 animals, with only 150 in Mexico

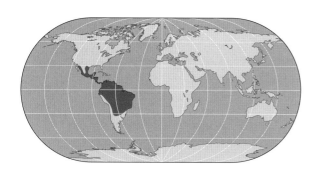

Ocelot

Felis pardalis

Ocelot numbers are now recovering from heavy losses caused by hunting and trapping. The animal's beautiful, lustrous fur was highly prized at a time when wearing fur was considered fashionable.

IN THE 1960S AND 1970S THE exquisitely patterned coat of the ocelot was a common sight on the fashionable streets of Paris, around racecourses in England, and in the chic restaurants of Berlin and New York. Unfortunately, the coats were being worn by people, not cats. Ocelot fur was so sought after that over 200,000 wild animals were killed every year to supply the demand, more than any other cat. Most of the dead animals were exported from South and Central America to Europe, where by the 1980s an ocelot fur coat could fetch in excess of $800,000. Ocelots are not small animals, but it can take a lot of them to make just one coat because the furrier has to find pieces of fur whose patterns match along the seams.

New Problems

Hunting almost drove the ocelot to extinction in many places, but the species is now widely protected. In some parts of its former range it appears to be on the increase. In other areas ocelots are facing new problems, mostly involving loss of habitat. Ocelots are highly adaptable cats. They eat almost any small- to medium-sized animal and live in habitats as varied as tropical forest, thorny scrub, and mountains. Their only consistent requirement is that the habitat includes some dense vegetation in which to hide during the day. In the states of Texas and Louisiana such thickets have become very rare. Most have been grubbed out for agriculture or lost due to grazing by cattle. The ocelots that once lived there have all but disappeared. It is believed that there may now only be about 100 wild Texas ocelots left in the United States, restricted to the extreme southwest of Texas.

Intensive Research

The plight of the ocelot has prompted a program of intensive research into the species. As a result, it is now better known than many other small cats. Studies of ocelots in the wild have shown that while most animals live solitary lives, they manage to maintain social ties with their neighbors.

Female ocelots occupy a private home range of up to 4.5 square miles (11 sq. km). Males have ranges of up to twice the size,

⊕ *The ocelot's striking coat provides effective camouflage among the dense vegetation of the rain forest—but at one time made it a target for fur hunters and trappers.*

which overlap with those of several females. Males and females meet to breed, but apart from that are rarely seen together. Raising the family is very much the female's responsibility. In the tropics seasonal changes in the availability of food are insignificant, so ocelots can breed at any time of year. In the north of the species' range, however, they mate in winter, so the kittens are born in spring when there is plenty of prey to support them.

There are usually just one or two kittens, rarely three, but they are extremely lively and demanding. It is often as much as their mother can do to keep her small family out of danger as they try to investigate their world. Infant mortality can be high, and adolescents are much more prone to misadventure than experienced adults. All this means that the overall rate of population increase is frustratingly slow, even where the ocelot receives special protection.

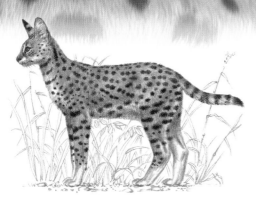

Common name Serval

Scientific name *Felis serval*

Family	Felidae
Order	Carnivora

Size Length head/body: 26–39 in (67–100 cm); tail length: 9–18 in (24–45 cm); height at shoulder: 21–24.5 in (54–62 cm)

Weight 20–40 lb (9–18 kg)

Key features Slender, long-limbed cat with longish neck and very large, rounded ears; coat is light beige to dark gold, pale on underside, and marked with variable black spots and streaks; black rings on tail

Habits Active by day or night; solitary and territorial; performs leaps when hunting, displaying, and as a means of seeing over long grass

Breeding One or 2 litters of 1–4 kittens born each year after gestation period of 74 days. Weaned at 6 months; sexually mature at 2 years. May live up to 20 years in captivity, 13 in the wild

Voice Growls, purrs, and shrill, far-carrying calls

Diet Mostly mice; also small mammals and birds

Habitat Riverside grasslands and reed beds; savanna regions, mountain grasslands

Distribution Most of sub-Saharan Africa, excluding Congo Basin and large deserts such as the Namib, Karroo, and Kalahari. Small outlying population in Morocco

Status Population: abundant; IUCN Endangered (Morroccan subspecies); CITES II. Common, but declining due to hunting and habitat loss

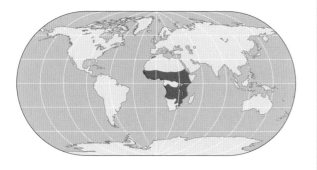

Serval

Felis serval

Resembling a small, slender leopard, the serval occurs over most of Africa, except in deserts and dense forest.

THE SERVAL HAS BEEN DESCRIBED as the "cat of spare parts," and with its huge ears, small face, and elongated legs it is easy to see why. Early European explorers were obviously puzzled by this unlikely animal's behavior as well as its appearance—the name serval derives from the Portuguese words for "wolf-deer" and presumably refers to the serval's predatory nature and its deerlike leaps and bounds.

Most servals are marked all over with large black spots, but some have much finer markings, more like freckles. Animals like this are sometimes called servalines; they were once thought to be a different species. Now, however, we know that speckle-coated individuals are just a genetic variation and that both spotted and speckly kittens can occur in the same litter.

Graceful Hunters

Despite its gawky appearance, the serval is far from awkward. Its long legs and neck are an adaptation to life among tall grass and reed stems, and its enormous ears act as highly sensitive dish antennae, rotating this way and that to pinpoint the tiniest sound.

Servals are efficient hunters and succeed in making a kill in about half of their attempts. This success rate is even higher at night, but servals adjust their daily activity to the behavior of their preferred prey. For example, if most of the rats in an area are active by day, then the servals will be too. Ground-dwelling prey are located mainly by sound, then attacked with a typical catlike pounce. Servals can also catch birds, leaping up to 10 feet (3 m) out of the grass to swat them to the ground with their front paws. The serval's long legs can also be used for scooping small animals out of burrows, and the serval has flexible wrists and hooked claws to assist this action. If there is shallow

water nearby, the serval may wade in to hunt for fish or frogs.

Leaping Displays

Servals occupy fairly small home ranges, which overlap considerably. However, each animal has a core area of personal territory, which other servals usually avoid. Males are more territorial than females and may mark their core area with urine over 500 times a day. Intruding males are treated to a highly conspicuous display of bouncing and leaping, but disputes rarely become aggressive. Courtship is brief, since females are only receptive for a day at a time. The kittens are born in the long grass and moved regularly from place to place. Both adults and young are vulnerable to predation by hyenas, dogs, and leopards. Baby servals are

born with small ears, but they grow rapidly. The youngsters learn to hunt by watching their mother. She will drive the males of her litter away almost as soon as they can feed themselves, but young females stick around a bit longer. When they do leave, they will often set up home not far away.

Servals are widespread throughout sub-Saharan Africa and remain common in many parts of their range. Even so, they have still suffered their share of persecution and have been eradicated from populated areas, including most of South Africa. Serval fur is not especially valuable in itself, but pelts are used in traditional African costumes and sometimes sold to gullible tourists as baby leopard or cheetah skins. Some tribes regard serval meat as a delicacy.

⤴ The serval's alert, attentive appearance is indicative of its efficient hunting techniques. The huge ears can pinpoint the faintest sound.

Common name
Wildcat

Scientific name *Felis silvestris*

Family	Felidae
Order	Carnivora
Size	Length head/body: 20–30 in (50–76 cm); tail length: 8–14 in (21–35 cm); height at shoulder: 15–22 in (38–56 cm)

Weight 6.6–17.6 lb (3–8 kg)

Key features Smallish cat with thick fur, very similar to a domestic tabby; tail noticeably bushy with blunt end

Habits Solitary; mainly active between dusk and dawn; excellent climber

Breeding Litters of 1–8 kittens born after gestation period of 61–68 days; births occur late spring in north, during rainy season in south, and year-round in tropics. Weaned at 30 days; sexually mature at 9–12 months. May live up to 15 years in captivity, fewer in the wild

Voice Catlike mewing, hissing, and screeching

Diet Mainly small mammals, especially rabbits and rodents; also birds, reptiles, and amphibians

Habitat Forests, scrub, and open country with rocky crevices and patchy vegetation

Distribution Scotland and southwestern Europe, including several Mediterranean islands; Africa (except for large deserts and tropical rain forests); Middle East and central and southern Asia, India, and north-central China

Status Population: widespread and common; IUCN Vulnerable (Scottish population); CITES II (Scottish population). Globally abundant, but some local populations now very small

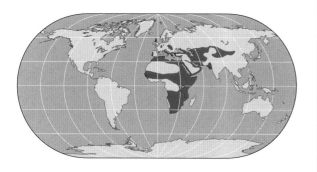

Wildcat

Felis silvestris

Wildcats are savage predators, yet one form has been domesticated for thousands of years and is much loved as a family pet the world over.

THE WILDCAT IS ONE OF THE most widespread members of the cat family, with a range extending from western Europe south to South Africa and east to India and China. Within its range, however, the species is split into many isolated populations, with some local variations in appearance, physiology, and behavior. European cats appear bigger than African cats because of their thicker coats, and gestation in European and central Asian cats is about a week longer than in their African cousins.

Nocturnal Predators

Wildcats live in a variety of habitats, but they do best where there are few people. They tend to be nocturnal and spend the day hiding in one of several dens within a home range of between 0.4 and 2 square miles (1 and 5 sq. km). In cooler climates they need to keep themselves warm in order to save energy. They will often spend time basking in the sun, either on the branch of a tree or on a secure rocky outcrop. By night they move around using regular pathways between favored hunting spots. They catch prey using a "stalk-and-pounce" technique. In Africa the diet is much the same all year round; in parts of Europe wildcats favor rabbits in spring when there are lots of babies to catch, and in the fall when the viral disease myxomatosis makes adults easy to attack. They also catch mice and voles, and often ambush birds feeding on the ground.

Males compete aggressively for the right to mate with a female, but then play no further part in raising their family. The young are born in a tree hollow or rock crevice where they depend on their mother's milk for the first month. After that they emerge from the den to play and follow their mother, who supplies

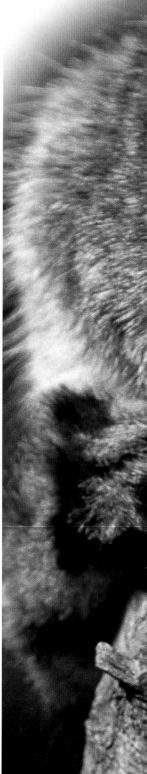

them with meat until they can catch their own prey. They disperse in the winter before the start of the breeding season, and some females may be mothers themselves before their first birthday. Males, however, rarely breed before they are two or three years old because of competition for females from older, more experienced cats.

Well-known Relative

The wildcat is the ancestor and closest relative of the domestic cat. The latter is thought to have appeared in Africa between 4 and 8 thousand years ago, a mere instant in evolutionary time. Sometimes the African wildcat is regarded as a separate species to other wildcats (yet still the origin of the domestic form). Other scientists consider wild and domestic cats to be the same species. It is certainly true that the two can interbreed successfully. In some parts of the wildcat's range so much hybridization is taking place that there may soon be no purebred wildcats left.

One of the most important differences between wildcats and their domestic relatives is temperament. True wildcats really are wild, elusive, and extremely ferocious. It is claimed they are impossible to tame. Indeed, they have every reason to detest humans. Studies of European wildcat populations show that up to 92 percent of all deaths are due to human interference, through hunting or persecution, accidental killing such as on roads, or in snares set for other animals. Wildcats are protected by law throughout Europe, but the expansion of human populations into previously unpopulated areas of wildcat habitat means they are unlikely to become common there ever again.

⏴ *Wildcats are generally nocturnal and spend the day hiding in dens. In cooler climates they need to keep themselves warm and will often spend time basking in the sun on a tree branch or rock.*

The Dog Family

The first doglike animals probably appeared in what is now North America about 38 million years ago. Several other groups of mammals evolved at the same time, but it was not until about 20 million years ago, in the Miocene period, that dogs became fully distinct from their closest relatives, the bears. By that time they had spread naturally all over the world except Antarctica and Australasia. More recently dogs have reached almost everywhere, assisted by the unstoppable advance of a single species—our own.

What Is a Dog?

Members of the dog family (domestic dogs and their relatives, including foxes and wolves) are "cursorial" animals, meaning they are built for running. Most species have a lightweight body, a long, bushy tail, and a deep chest to accommodate efficient lungs. The legs are long and slender, with most species having five digits on the

front feet and four on the back. The claws of the fifth front toes are separated from their pads and positioned higher up the leg—they are known as dewclaws. Unlike bears, dogs walk on their toes, not the whole foot.

Wild dogs range in size from the diminutive fennec fox, weighing little more than 3 pounds (1.4 kg), to the great gray wolf, a large specimen that can weigh 170 pounds (77 kg). The head of a dog is typically long, with well-developed jaws, forward-facing eyes, and prominent ears. Dogs are smart animals and have a keen sense of hearing, good eyesight, and a highly developed sense of smell. Hearing is especially acute in the African bat-eared fox, which uses its huge ears to listen for the movements of tiny creatures under the soil: Up to 80 percent of the bat-eared fox's diet consists of termites.

The dog's teeth include long, stabbing canines and sharp, biting incisors. The molar teeth are sharp, too, for chopping up meat. Dogs have 42 teeth, 10 more than humans. Most species specialize in eating flesh, but they can also cope with other foods. Although all dogs belong to the order Carnivora, very few feed entirely on other animals. Most take a variety of prey and supplement their diet with fruit and other plant matter. The teeth of the bat-eared fox differ from those of other dogs, being smaller and more numerous. This unusual species also has extra muscles to allow the fast chewing movements required to eat very small, active prey such as insects.

Where Dogs Live

Different kinds of wild dogs have exploited a huge range of habitats from hot deserts (dingo and fennec fox) to the high open grasslands of the arctic tundra and ice fields (gray wolf and Arctic fox). Dogs are usually creatures of open spaces such as grassland, prairies, or

Family Canidae: 10 genera, 36 species	
Canis	8 species, including domestic dog (*C. familiaris*); gray wolf (*C. lupus*); coyote (*C. latrans*); black-backed jackal (*C. mesomelas*); dingo (*C. dingo*); Ethiopian wolf (*C. simensis*)
Nyctereutes	1 species, raccoon dog (*N. procyonoides*)
Speothos	1 species, bush dog (*S. venaticus*)
Chrysocyon	1 species, maned wolf (*C. brachyurus*)
Cuon	1 species, dhole (*C. alpinus*)
Lycaon	1 species, African wild dog (*L. pictus*)
Vulpes	12 species, including red fox (*V. vulpes*); Arctic fox (*V. lagopus*); fennec fox (*V. (Fennecus) zerda*); swift fox (*V. velox*); cape fox (*V. chama*); Rüppell's fox (*V. rüppelli*); Blanford's fox (*V. cana*); Indian fox (*V. bengalensis*); corsac fox (*V. corsac*)
Urocyon	2 species, gray fox (*U. cinereoargenteus*); island gray fox (*U. littoralis*)
Dusicyon	8 species, excluding the recently extinct Falkland Island wolf (*D. australis*)
Otocyon	1 species, bat-eared fox (*O. megalotis*)

⊙ *Dholes are Asian wild dogs. In many respects their lifestyle resembles that of the African wild dog, with group living, cooperative hunting, and shared care of the young forming the basis of the society.*

⊕ Eight species of fox depicted in a dash-and-swipe attack on a bird, shown left to right to reflect their west to east order of distribution: gray fox (1); swift fox (2); cape fox (3); fennec fox (4); Rüppell's fox (5); Blanford's fox (6); Indian fox (7); and corsac fox (8). Foxes have been characterized as solitary hunters and foragers, but radio tracking has shown that fox societies can be quite complex. Some foxes are monogamous; others live in groups generally made up of an adult male and two vixens (female foxes). There is no evidence indicating that vixens join other groups, so it is likely that the female members of a group are all related.

1

2

3

4

SEE ALSO Fox, Swift **2**:68; Dog, African Wild **2**:78; Dingo **2**:80; Thylacine **10**:36

Ethiopian wolf pups with their mother. The pups have a close bond with their mother, but other pack members will usually help feed them once they have been weaned.

light woodland. However, a few species, such as the bush dog of South America, have adapted to life among dense vegetation.

Dogs were taken to Australia about 4,000 years ago, and they have accompanied humans to many other islands since then. They have reached Antarctica, where they were used to pull the sleds of many of the early explorers. Dogs have even been sent into space!

Lifestyle

Dogs were actually the first mammals to be domesticated. Perhaps the pups were originally taken in and reared as pets. Soon it became clear that dogs were useful and could help with hunting and tracking, putting their keen sense of smell to use and helping make up for the poorly developed tracking and sniffing abilities of humans. Dogs can carry small loads and in some places are even used as food. There are now many millions of domestic dogs in the world. With our help the dog has become one of the most successful of all mammal species.

Dogs are generally long-lived (10 years or more), but are born small and virtually helpless. The young require a prolonged period of parental care to learn skills such as hunting. Some dogs live alone except when breeding, while others are more gregarious and live in social groups called packs. The maned wolf of South America lives in faithful pairs, while gray wolves and African wild dogs are highly social, living in packs dominated by a breeding pair whose offspring are cared for by the entire group. Dogs communicate using body postures and facial expressions, as well as a variety of barks, yelps, growls, whines, and howls. They also leave messages in the form of special scent deposited with urine or feces.

"Man's Best Friend" or Big, Bad Wolf?

Domestic dogs are classed as a single species despite the extreme diversity of forms in over 400 recognized breeds. They are generally regarded as descendants of the gray wolf, whose naturally social and cooperative behavior transferred easily to a

The now extinct Falkland Island wolf.

human "pack leader." The earliest remains that can be reliably classified as *Canis familiaris*, the domestic dog, were found in Iraq and appear to be about 12,000 years old. Initially tamed and kept as working animals—mainly for use in hunting—dogs have probably been valued as companion animals for several thousand years. Ironically, some of the same qualities that make dogs so useful and popular (their intelligence and hunting skills) give many wild dogs a bad name. Foxes, dingoes, and wolves of almost every kind are persecuted in at least part of their range. Several species are threatened with extinction, and at least one, the Falkland Island wolf, has already been exterminated—in that case by sheep farmers.

Most dogs are nocturnal or crepuscular (active at dawn and dusk). However, nearly all species can be active during the day in places where they have no need to fear attack from humans, who are responsible for some large-scale losses.

7

8

5

6

Common name Gray wolf (timber wolf)

Scientific name *Canis lupus*

Family	Canidae
Order	Carnivora

Size Length head/body: 35–56 in (89–142 cm); tail length: 12–20 in (30–51 cm); height at shoulder: 23–28 in (58–77 cm)

Weight 22–175 lb (10–80 kg). Male larger than female

Key features Large, long-legged dog with thick fur and bushy tail; fur usually gray, although color varies with distribution

Habits Social, although sometimes solitary; more or less nocturnal; hunts communally to bring down prey up to 10 times its own weight

Breeding One to 11 (average 6) pups born in a den after gestation period of 63 days. Weaned at 5 weeks; sexually mature at 2 years. May live up to 16 years in captivity, rarely more than 13 in the wild

Voice Growls, barks, whines, and howls

Diet Mainly large mammal prey, including deer, moose, muskox, mountain sheep, bison, beavers, and hares

Habitat Almost anywhere from tundra to scrub, grassland, mountains, and forest

Distribution Northern Hemisphere

Status Population: many thousands; IUCN Vulnerable; CITES I (India, Pakistan, Nepal, Bhutan); elsewhere CITES II. Now more stable following centuries of persecution

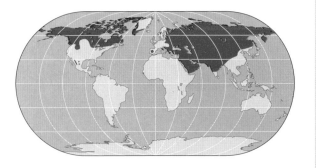

Gray Wolf

Canis lupus

Wolves are intelligent and adaptable creatures, often living in close-knit family groups. Human attitudes to wolves range from deep respect to outright hostility, fueled by chilling folk tales of their wickedness.

THE GRAY WOLF IS THE LARGEST species of dog. It once lived throughout the Northern Hemisphere in all but the most extreme tropical and desert habitats. Only one other mammal has a greater natural range or lives in a wider variety of habitats—our own species. Persecution by humans led to a dramatic decline in wolf numbers worldwide over the last 300 years, and the species has become extinct over much of its former range. It is now associated only with areas of wilderness. Wolves disappeared altogether from Britain in the 18th century and from Japan and much of western Europe in the following 200 years.

Eradication Program

In North America the gray wolf was the chief target of a prolonged campaign of predator eradication that began soon after the arrival of European settlers. Wolves were shot and trapped in such numbers that by 1940 there were none left in the western United States, and numbers elsewhere were in serious decline. More recent methods of control include poisoning and sport hunting from aircraft. Similar eradication programs in the former Soviet Union reduced wolf numbers there by about 70 percent. In other parts of Asia the wolf is now rare. The Mexican wolf is officially listed by the IUCN as Extinct in the Wild, with only about 140 remaining in captivity.

More recently, however, studies of wolf populations have convinced biologists that far from being a scourge of the land, wolves are in fact an important stabilizing influence on wilderness ecosystems. Such discoveries, along with a growing sense of responsibility toward wildlife in general, have prompted several wolf

⊕ Gray wolves from different geographical areas may vary in size and appearance. Those living in arctic and mountainous regions, for example, are much larger than their relatives in the hot, dry scrublands of Arabia.

Folklore: Who's Afraid of the Big, Bad Wolf?

Wolves have long been the subject of myths and legends. Stories such as *Little Red Riding Hood* and *The Three Little Pigs* cast wolves as cold-blooded killers of men and domestic animals. On the other hand, the legend of Romulus and Remus —the babies raised by wolves— and Kipling's *Jungle Book* stories portray wolves as wise and devoted parents. In reality the wolf is all these things and more.

conservation projects around the world. Several European populations have now been saved from extinction, and the range of the wolf in North America is increasing slowly. In most places where man and wolf still live side by side there is now an uneasy truce enforced by laws protecting the wolf from direct persecution, but giving livestock owners some rights to protect their property. Nevertheless, many country people are not happy to share their land with wolves and want them shot or trapped. Efforts to reintroduce wolves to Yellowstone National Park have also run into difficulties with hostile residents in surrounding areas.

Geographical Differences

Not surprisingly for such a widespread species, wolves from different geographical areas vary considerably in size, appearance, and behavior. The biggest wolves live in large packs in the tundra regions of Canada, Alaska, and Russia. Their relatives in the hot, dry scrublands of Arabia are smaller and more likely to live alone or in small groups.

The size of a wolf pack is controlled largely by the size of its most regular prey. Lone wolves do well where most of their food comes from small prey, carrion, or raiding human refuse. Where deer are the main prey, packs of five to seven animals are usual.

However, pack sizes may be larger still where wolves feed on very big prey. In the Isle Royale National Park in Lake Superior, for example, where the animals feed almost exclusively on moose, packs may include more than 20 animals.

Selective Predation

Wolves normally hunt old, young, weak, or disabled prey and soon give up an attack if the animal is able to defend itself or make a quick getaway. In fact, only about 8 percent of wolf hunts end in a kill, which is why it is highly unlikely that wolf predation does any real harm to prey populations as was once feared.

A large wolf needs to eat an average of 5.5 pounds (2.5 kg) of meat every day, but will often go for several days without food. However, when a kill is made, it makes up for any such lean periods by "wolfing" up to 20 pounds (9 kg) in a single meal. A large prey animal may keep a pack well fed for several

days. During the time they are not actively feeding, the wolves may rest near the carcass to defend it from scavengers.

Wolf attacks on humans are rare. In North America, for example, there are no fully documented cases of unprovoked attacks on people by healthy wolves. However, wolves can and do attack livestock. Sheep and cattle are, after all, close relatives of the wolf's natural prey and yet far easier to catch and kill because generations of domestication have made them virtually incapable of defending themselves. They are large, meaty, and prone to panic, and are often penned in with no hope of escape. Even so, it would rarely take more than the sight of a human to cause the wolves to abandon the hunt and run away.

Sibling Care

A wolf pack is made up of a single breeding pair and their offspring of the previous one or two years. The nonbreeding members of the pack are usually young animals. They are prevented from breeding by the dominant pair, but help care for their young siblings. In areas where good wolf habitat is plentiful, young

⬆ *The size of a wolf pack is usually determined by the size of available prey. For example, when deer are the main food source, packs of five to seven are common. Wolves preying on larger animals, such as moose, often belong to packs of 20 or more.*

Reintroduction

In 1995, after years of careful planning and much controversy, 31 Canadian-born gray wolves were released into Yellowstone National Park. The park contains over 17 million acres (7 million ha) of prime wolf habitat and also supports large herds of elk. The relocated wolves have thrived since their introduction, as have those released in other locations in Montana and Idaho. The interests of local ranchers are protected in that they are compensated for wolf attacks on their livestock. In addition, farmers are now permitted to shoot wolves on their own land. In the first four years of the program nine wolves were shot legally.

The success of the Yellowstone project has encouraged conservationists to consider reintroducing the wolf elsewhere. One highly controversial plan is to release captive-bred wolves in Scotland, a country that has not seen wild wolves for 300 years. The problem with the idea is that islands where wolves could be out of the way of humans are too small to support a viable population. Yet on the mainland there are too many people and sheep for the wolves to live without causing trouble.

A gray wolf pup at the entrance to its den. On average, a litter contains about six pups.

wolves may leave their parents' pack as early as 12 months of age. Some stay with the family for a further season; but by the time they are fully mature at 22 months, they will move on. Dispersing animals may live on the edge of their parents' territory until a suitable mate comes along. Other young wolves scatter widely in search of a mate and territory of their own.

Territorial Howling

The pack occupies a territory of anything from 8 to 5,200 square miles (20 to 13,000 sq. km), the exact size varying according to the number of wolves and quality of habitat. All pack members help defend the territory, and they will travel to every part of it at least once a month, moving in single file along regular routes. They mark their territory with scents, scratches, and long sessions of howling. In open country wolf howls can be heard up to 10 miles (16 km) away, even by human ears. When wolves from neighboring packs do meet, the

encounters often lead to serious fights in which one or more animals may be fatally wounded. To minimize the risk of such incidents, the wolves usually leave a kind of buffer zone of seldom-visited land around the edge of their territory. Such areas also serve as a kind of reservoir for prey, which is only exploited in times of food shortage.

All wolves are highly adaptable. While the social structure of a pack may stay the same for many years, individuals are able to switch roles with surprising ease. The dominant (or alpha) male leads the pack and is responsible for initiating hunts or other movements. If he dies or is absent for long periods, the alpha female takes on the leadership role until a new alpha male moves in. Subordinate wolves rise to dominance almost as soon as an alpha wolf dies, and both sexes are capable of rearing older cubs on their own if their mate dies.

⬆ *Wolves communicate using body language and facial expressions. Above, a defensive threatening posture (1); a submissive greeting (2); and an offensive threatening pose (3).*

Common name Coyote

Scientific name *Canis latrans*

Family	Canidae
Order	Carnivora

Size Length head/body: 30–39 in (76–100 cm); tail length: 12–19 in (30–48 cm); height at shoulder: about 24 in (60 cm)

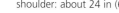

Weight 15.5–44 lb (7–20 kg). Male slightly larger than female

Key features Typical wolf but smaller and slighter in build than gray wolf; ears large and pointed; muzzle narrow; fur shaggy and usually a shade of beige or gray; paler on belly, but darkening to black on tip of tail

Habits Mostly nocturnal, but can be active at any time of day; some migrate into mountains in summer; less social than gray wolf

Breeding Litters of 2–12 (average 6) born in spring after gestation period of 63 days. Weaned at 5–6 weeks; sexually mature at 1 or 2 years. May live up to 21 years in captivity, usually fewer than 15 in the wild

Voice Wide repertoire of barks, whines, and howls

Diet Carnivorous; mostly mammals, including rabbits, woodchucks, rodents, and deer; also carrion

Habitat Grasslands and prairie, scrub, and forest

Distribution North America

Status Population: abundant. Common and widespread; hunted for fur and as a pest

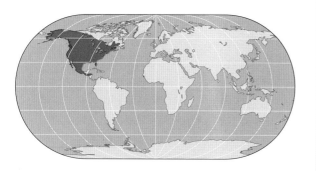

Coyote

Canis latrans

Opportunistic and resilient, the North American coyote is the archetypal predator. The species continues to thrive throughout its range, despite centuries of persecution by humans.

THE COYOTE IS ONE OF THE WORLD'S most successful carnivores. The species occupies a vast range, and local populations seem able to adapt to a wide variety of habitats. The size of the animals, their diet, and their social structures are all flexible in order to make the most of different environmental conditions wherever they live. Coyotes continue to do well despite centuries of intensive persecution by humans.

Coyote Persecution

Millions of coyotes have been killed for their fur and to protect game and livestock, especially sheep. Young coyotes are killed in their dens, and the adults are trapped or shot by marksmen on foot or in aircraft. Poisoning used to be a major method of coyote control. It was outlawed in 1972, partly because it was considered cruel, but also because many other species were harmed accidentally by eating poison meant for coyotes. Coyote predation still costs farmers millions of dollars a year. While there is no evidence that the population is seriously threatened by the ongoing persecution, the control of coyotes has become highly controversial. Recent investigations suggest that in most states coyote predation on livestock is not as common as people thought.

Ironically, the arrival of European settlers in North America has done more to extend the coyote's range than to control its numbers. Before human settlement coyotes were restricted to the plains of central North America by the lack of suitable habitat elsewhere and the presence of wolves, which were bigger and better adapted to forest life. As the human population expanded westward, landscapes changed. The forests were felled and replaced

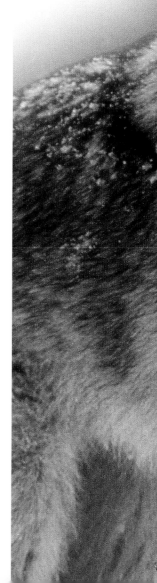

⤵ *A coyote howls in a snowstorm in Yellowstone National Park. Its long howl is only one of a varied repertoire of calls.*

SEE ALSO Wolf, Gray **2**:54; Fox, Red **2**:64; Woodchuck **7**:50

with pasture and arable land. Human fear of wolves meant that the coyote's main competitor was eradicated from many states in a short space of time. The coyote was presented with an unprecedented opportunity for expansion, and today the species occupies all but the extreme northeast of the continent.

Hybridization

In places where advancing coyotes encountered remaining populations of gray and red wolves, the species interbred. The resulting hybridization almost proved disastrous for the red wolf, purebred examples of which became so rare that in 1975 the remaining population had to be taken into captivity for its own protection. Unfortunately, after 25 years of captive breeding and subsequent release onto coyote-free reserves, there are still fewer than 300 red wolves left in the world.

By contrast, coyotes are so numerous that interbreeding has done little to dilute their gene pool. In fact, evidence suggests that an injection of wolf genes has resulted in larger coyotes in Canada better adapted to life on the tundra. Even where there are no wolves, coyotes have gotten bigger, partly as a

The Coyotes Come to Town

Coyotes are adaptable animals. They are capable of living in a wide variety of habitats, including suburban areas. As cities expand, many animals die out, being unable to adjust to the new conditions. Not so the coyote! The species is often seen in the outskirts of cities like Denver, Houston, and Boise, and is particularly familiar in Los Angeles. It appears that coyotes did not invade Los Angeles, but merely stayed put as the city spread around them. Los Angeles is especially suitable because there are many scrub-filled ravines, large gardens, and other relatively undisturbed areas where they can live, emerging to feed on trash, food scraps, and other urban animals. The red fox has made a similar success of urban living in parts of Britain.

result of improved food resources. Coyotes living in the Mexican desert average about 28 pounds (13 kg). Those that have colonized Alaska regularly exceed 42 pounds (20 kg).

The coyote is smaller than a wolf, but substantially bigger than a fox. It can be difficult to distinguish from a wolf, but the narrow snout, long ears, and small feet are identifying features. Another useful clue, especially at a distance, is the tail. It is long and brushy like that of most other wild dogs. However, when running, the coyote carries its tail in a low sweep, not high like a wolf or straight out like a fox, nor curled like some domestic dogs. Other less obvious differences are clues to the coyote's lifestyle. A coyote's skull has a pronounced central ridge running from front to back (called a sagittal crest), which allows for the attachment of powerful jaw muscles that are much bigger than those of a fox. The coyote has crushing molar teeth and long, pointed canines, designed for tearing and chewing chunks off large prey. Foxes, on the other hand, have more pointed teeth, less muscular jaws, and feed on smaller animals.

Coyotes are out-and-out carnivores, with the flesh of mammals providing at least 90 percent of their food. The exact composition of their diet varies with habitat and season, from rabbits and rodents on grassland to mostly deer in the forests of Minnesota. Some coyotes have learned rudimentary fishing techniques, while others occasionally catch and eat birds. Fruit and vegetables are eaten in season. Hunting techniques vary depending on the prey, but a large proportion of the animals caught are old, sick, or immature. Small prey are stalked and pounced on from above, while large animals may be chased over long distances. The coyote is one of the fastest predators in the Americas, able to run down prey at speeds of up to 40 miles per hour (64 km/h).

Hunting as a pack is a definite advantage when chasing large prey over a distance, since different members take turns leading the chase until the quarry tires. Coyotes tend to live in packs only where large prey animals, such as deer, are concentrated in an area. Packs usually consist of three to seven closely related animals. Larger groups sometimes gather around a temporary food source, such as a large carcass, but are not assembled for long. In less productive habitats coyotes live in pairs or alone and hunt small animals over a wide area.

⊕ *A coyote pack defends a carcass on the edge of its territory. Three pack members (1) feed while the dominant male (2) threatens an intruder (3), who assumes a defensive threat posture. Another male (4) backs up his leader, but shows less aggression. Another trespasser (5) looks on while other coyotes (6) wait in their own territory for the pack to leave.*

Hunting Partnerships

Cooperative hunting is not unusual among carnivores—lions do it, and so do some species of otters and dogs. Coyotes sometimes hunt in packs, but by far their most remarkable teamwork is performed with an unlikely partner: the American badger. The two animals form an alliance and use their combined skills to catch prey that would otherwise escape them. The coyote sniffs out small burrowing mammals under the soil and waits patiently while the badger uses its powerful forelimbs and huge claws to dig them out. The badger's sense of smell is not good enough to detect buried prey, and the coyote's small feet mean that digging is a slow and laborious exercise. Once caught, the prey is shared amicably between the partners. Cooperation between the two animals has evolved over generations and works because both benefit equally.

Male coyotes have large home ranges of up to 32 square miles (80 sq. km), which can often overlap with those of other males. Female territories rarely exceed 6.5 square miles (17 sq. km), but are generally exclusive, each female having her own territory. Coyotes seem to choose obvious landmarks such as streams and tree lines to define their territories, and they mark them with scent in urine and feces.

Courtship

A single female may be courted by several males over a period of two or three months in spring. However, once she has chosen one male to be her mate, the relationship may last several years, sometimes for life. The female bears just one litter a year, but it can include 10 or more pups (litters of 19 pups have been recorded, but it is highly unlikely that all could survive).

The average litter contains five to seven pups. In good habitat pups are tended by both parents and one or more elder sisters. Helpers only tend to stay with their parents where there is no shortage of large prey, and so their presence may be more important in defending the young and the den than in obtaining food.

Coyote pups begin to eat regurgitated meat at just three weeks old, and by the time they are six weeks old they no longer need their mother's milk. They put on weight fast and are fully grown by the age of nine months. Male offspring disperse at this time, while females may stay behind for a further two or three years. Dispersing coyotes travel an average of 18 miles (30 km) from the den where they were born, but tagging studies show that some travel hundreds of miles before settling down to raise a family of their own.

⬆ As a form of greeting, coyotes will often rear up on their hind legs and nuzzle each other's face. Aggressive encounters begin in a similar way, but may develop into a wrestling match, with rolling and biting.

Common name Black-backed jackal

Scientific name *Canis mesomelas*

Family	Canidae
Order	Carnivora
Size	Length head/body: 18–35.5 in (45–90 cm); tail length: 12–19 in (30–48 cm); height at shoulder: 10–16 in (26–40 cm)
	Weight 13–29 lb (6–13.5 kg)
Key features	Small and foxlike with slender legs, pointed face, and large triangular ears; coat rough and reddish-gray, except for dark patch on back extending to tip of tail
Habits	Active at any time of day; lives alone or in small family groups; territorial
Breeding	One to 8 (usually 4) young born at the start of the rainy season after gestation period of 60 days. Weaned at 8–9 weeks; sexually mature at 11 months. May live up to 14 years in captivity, usually fewer than 8 in the wild
Voice	Eerie-sounding barks and howls
Diet	Varied: mammalian prey (from mice to small antelope); also dead meat; invertebrates such as beetles, grubs, and worms; plant material
Habitat	Tropical grassland and open woodland
Distribution	Two distinct ranges; the first includes parts of Kenya, Tanzania, Somalia, and Ethiopia; the other falls in parts of South Africa, Namibia, Botswana, Angola, and Zimbabwe
Status	Population: abundant and common; persecuted as vermin, especially by sheep farmers

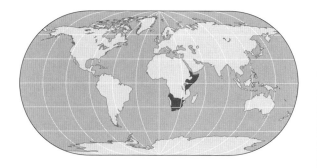

Black-Backed Jackal

Canis mesomelas

The black-backed jackal, with its distinctive dark saddle patch, is found in two separate populations in Africa, divided by the desert at the southern end of the Great African Rift Valley.

OF THE FOUR SPECIES OF JACKAL living in Africa the black-backed is the most distinctive. It has a well-defined black or dark-gray saddle patch running down the length of its body. Jackals are small African wolves. They are slightly smaller than most other wild members of the genus *Canis*, but in other respects very similar.

Divided Populations

Black-backed jackals occur in two distinct populations separated by a belt of inhospitable land at the southern end of the Great African Rift Valley. Both populations occupy similar kinds of country and do best in areas of grassland and scrub that are generally too dry for other wild dogs to cope with. In such harsh conditions prey animals are generally smaller and harder to find than in wetter areas, and the black-backed jackal has to cover a wide area to find enough to eat. A typical black-backed jackal inhabits a home range of between 4 and 12 square miles (10 and 30 sq. km), with the largest ranges belonging to young adults who go the extra distance in the hope of finding a suitable mate.

Once they have successfully paired, jackals remain with the same mate for many years, often until one of them dies. Both males and females defend their joint territory, marking out its borders with urine. Within a territory there will be several dens, usually converted from aardvark burrows or dug into termite mounds. Burrows have several entrances (a useful safety precaution, since young jackals can easily fall victim to a number of larger predators, including lions, domestic dogs, and birds of

⊕ A black-backed jackal resting in the shade. Jackals are small African wolves and are not as large as most other wild members of the genus Canis.

prey). The young are born in a secure den where they spend the first three or four weeks of their lives under the watchful eyes of both parents. As soon as they are able to see and walk any distance, they are hurried away to a new den. Switching dens happens repeatedly, making it more difficult for predators to find them. Young jackals may never spend more than a few days in the same place until they are old enough to defend themselves. The young are first weaned onto partially digested, regurgitated meat, but by the age of three months they are able to consume whole prey.

Jackal Helpers

The young of other jackal species tend to leave their parents' territory by the time they are one year old. By contrast, the offspring of black-backed jackals, especially the females, often remain with their parents for a year or two, helping rear the next litter of pups. Larger family groups are another adaptation to harsher, drier environments where it can take three or four adults to care for the pups and find enough food to rear them successfully.

Jackals are omnivorous They will catch and eat a wide variety of wild prey and will also take advantage of seasonally available food such as fruit, eggs, and young animals. Unfortunately,

the latter include spring lambs, and jackals have such a bad reputation for attacking them that they are usually killed on sight around sheep farms. The jackal's reputation means it probably gets the blame for kills made by other animals too, including domestic dogs. Some farmers put special collars on their sheep that deliver a lethal dose of poison to a jackal that attempts an attack on a flock.

Jackals are also hunted for fur and meat. Outside reserves and wildlife parks they receive no protection from persecution. Not surprisingly, they are wary of humans and quick to run away if they are disturbed. However, they can adapt well to life on the edges of towns, where they become almost completely nocturnal, coming out at night in order to avoid encounters with people.

⊕ *Black-backed jackal pups are born in an underground den where they are relatively safe from predators such as lions and birds of prey.*

Common name Red fox

Scientific name *Vulpes vulpes*

Family	Canidae
Order	Carnivora
Size	Length head/body: 18–35.5 in (45–90 cm); tail length: 12–21.5 in (30–55 cm); height at shoulder: up to 14 in (36 cm)
	Weight 7–31 lb (3–14 kg)

Key features Typical fox with long, narrow body ending in thick, brushy tail; pointed muzzle and ears; neat legs and feet; fur typically red, but varies from deep gold to dark brown, fading to white on muzzle, chest, and belly; often darker on legs; black and pale variants known

Habits Mostly nocturnal; sometimes lives in family groups, but usually hunts alone; nonbreeding males are solitary

Breeding Litters of 1–12 (usually 3–7) cubs born in spring after gestation period of 51–53 days. Weaned at 8–10 weeks; sexually mature at 10 months. May live up to 12 years in captivity, rarely more than 5 in the wild

Voice Barks, whines, yelps, screams, excited "gekkering" when playing

Diet Omnivorous; rodents and other small mammals; also insects, worms, and fruit

Habitat Diverse; includes farmland, forest, grassland, moorland, tundra, and urban areas

Distribution Europe and North America; also parts of Africa and Asia; introduced to Australia

Status Population: abundant. Persecuted as vermin; also hunted for sport

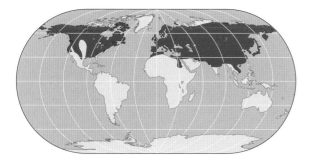

Red Fox

Vulpes vulpes

The red fox is one of the most widespread, and certainly one of the most adaptable, members of the dog family. It even rivals the gray wolf in terms of global distribution.

RED FOXES LIVE WILD IN NORTH America, Europe, Asia, and Africa, and have become widespread in Australia and on many islands to which they have been introduced. There is considerable variation in size and appearance throughout the range, with the largest foxes occurring in Europe. The typical red fox coat is a deep red-brown, with white on the muzzle, chest, belly, and tail tip, and black on the legs. In North America, however, there are many distinct color varieties, with up to 20 percent of red foxes being black or silver. Other varieties include so-called "cross foxes," which are basically red with a cross-shaped mark of darker fur on the shoulders. "Samson foxes" have coats that lack the normal long guard hairs and therefore look somewhat fluffier than usual.

Misrepresented

Throughout their huge geographical range foxes are loved and loathed in almost equal measure. It is difficult not to admire an animal so smart and adaptable that it is able to live almost anywhere that people can. The fox features frequently in folk tales and fairy stories, and its glorious pelt is valued as an expensive fashion accessory. However, the animal is traditionally detested by farmers and is persecuted throughout much of its range because of its predatory habits and the risk of transmitting rabies. Foxes are trapped, shot, and hunted almost everywhere they occur, and yet they still manage to thrive.

Foxes' diets and their hunting and foraging techniques vary as much as their habitat. In temperate climates in late summer many foxes exist almost entirely on sugary fruits, such as blackberries and apples. On warm, humid

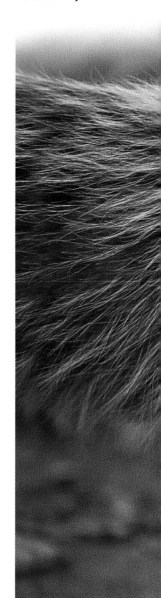

⊕ *A red fox holds an Arctic ground squirrel firmly in its jaws. The fox's sharp features and smart nature contribute to its reputation as a wanton predator. But contrary to popular opinion, foxes rarely kill more than they need.*

SEE ALSO Raccoon, Common **1**:22; Dog, African Wild **2**:78; Rabbit, European **8**:68

evenings in summer when earthworms come to the surface on open grassland and pasture, a fox can eat enough in an hour to keep it going for the whole day. At other times hunting is more intensive, and foxes will stalk, chase, and pounce on prey, including voles, rabbits, frogs, and birds. Ever the opportunist, a fox will also take advantage of roadkills and refuse. Excess food is usually stored—bones and bits of meat are buried in the ground to be dug up and eaten later, maggots and all. Rotten meat does not appear to do foxes any harm.

Chicken Runs

Foxes are messy eaters, and food remains are often scattered widely, but little is actually wasted. Contrary to popular opinion, foxes are not wanton killers and will rarely kill more than they need. Stories of foxes running amok in chicken runs and killing dozens of birds at a time have more to do with the unnatural conditions in which chickens are kept than the fox's killer instincts. In a run where chickens live at high density and have no way of escaping, a fox cannot simply make a kill and slink away to eat in peace. A flock of panicking birds causing mayhem all around sends the fox into a frenzy. As long as the chicken farmer ensures his enclosures are fox-proof, the problem does not arise.

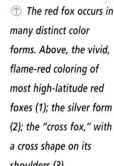

⊕ *The red fox occurs in many distinct color forms. Above, the vivid, flame-red coloring of most high-latitude red foxes (1); the silver form (2); the "cross fox," with a cross shape on its shoulders (3).*

Communal Lifestyle

Until recently foxes were thought to be solitary animals. They are certainly territorial and tend to hunt alone. However, in the privacy of their breeding dens the story can be quite different. A single communal territory can be home to as many as six adult foxes: one dominant male (the dog-fox) and up to five vixens (females). The vixens are apparently always related, each one either a sister, mother, or daughter to the others. The male usually mates with just one of the vixens, occasionally two if the habitat is productive enough to support an extra litter.

Breeding vixens are dominant over all the others. Status within a group is often established when the vixens are very young, long before they reach breeding age, and is reinforced continually. The dominant vixen is sometimes aggressive, sometimes friendly and reassuring, but her mood can change in an instant. Her subordinates are always ready to adopt cowering, submissive postures and to make themselves scarce when she chooses to remind them who is boss. Subordinate females seem to take great pride in caring for the dominant vixen's litter and compete for the privilege of baby-sitting.

Red Fox Cubs

Baby foxes are born in litters of one to 12, the average number varying according to the quality of habitat. The cubs are born blind but furry, and each weighs between 2 and 6 ounces (57 and 170 g). To begin with, their fur is dark chocolate brown, and their eyes, which open after two weeks, are blue. By the time the youngsters are one month old and ready to leave the safety of the breeding den for the first time, they have already begun to look more like foxes. Their fur lightens, their eyes turn brown, and their muzzles are longer and more pointed.

⊕ *Urban foxes make a good living feeding on refuse and bird-feeder leftovers, and by killing rats, pigeons, and other town-dwelling wildlife. Often the pickings are so rich that foxes in towns and cities live at much higher densities than they ever manage in the countryside.*

A young fox's first taste of meat is usually in the form of partially digested scraps coughed up by its mother. Later the cub's milk teeth drop out and are replaced by the adult dentition. The jaws and teeth are strengthened by chewing on bones, sticks, and other objects, and the cub's coordination and hunting skills are developed by hour on hour of boisterous play with its siblings. Adult foxes retain a playful streak, and games can involve the whole family in a noisy rough-and-tumble.

Habitat Requirements

Young females may stay with the family group, but males always disperse, traveling about 30 miles (48 km) or sometimes farther, to establish their own territory. The size of a fox's territory depends on the quality of the habitat and especially on the availability of food. Ideal fox habitat has a selection of different habitat types: Areas of woodland and pasture crisscrossed with hedgerows and the odd garden are ideal. Sometimes a fox can find all it needs in a territory of about 25 acres (10 ha). In less hospitable habitats, such as the Canadian tundra, a fox may require a hundred times as much space to supply its needs. Territories are diligently marked with urine and droppings.

⬆ *A female red fox with a cub. The cubs are ready to leave the safety of the breeding den at about one month. They can fend for themselves at six months and breed at 10 months.*

Deadly Virus

One of the most serious and widespread threats to foxes other than human persecution is the rabies virus. Rabies is found in much of the world's fox population, except in Britain, whose strict quarantine laws have kept the disease from becoming established. In continental Europe rabies has been largely eliminated from the fox population in several countries by using special vaccines distributed in baits, which the wild foxes eat. Vaccination programs reduce the threat of rabies because the disease dies out when there are enough foxes in the population that are immune to it. The method is expensive but humane and can be very effective as long as enough baits are distributed.

Common name Swift fox
(kit fox)

Scientific name *Vulpes velox*

Family	Canidae
Order	Carnivora
Size	Length head/body: 15–21 in (38–52 cm); tail length: 9–14 in (22–35 cm); height at shoulder: 12 in (30 cm)
Weight	4–7 lb (2–3 kg)
Key features	Similar to red fox; winter coat grayish-beige with pale undersides and rich orange-brown on legs, tail, and flanks; summer coat shorter and darker; bushy tail tipped with black and slightly shorter than in other foxes
Habits	Active at night; social, bold, and tame
Breeding	Three to 6 young born in spring after gestation period of 50–60 days. Weaned at 6–7 weeks; sexually mature at 10 months. May live up to 14 years in captivity, usually fewer than 6 in the wild
Voice	Quiet yelps and barks
Diet	Small mammals, especially rabbits, pikas, and rodents; also birds, lizards, amphibians, insects, and occasionally plant material
Habitat	Prairie and grassland
Distribution	Scattered populations across central plains of the U.S. and Canada
Status	Population: low thousands; IUCN Endangered (northern subspecies), elsewhere Lower Risk: conservation dependent; CITES I (northern subspecies)

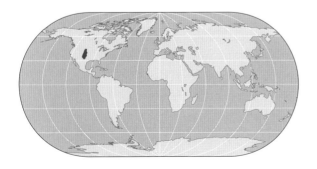

Swift Fox

Vulpes velox

The attractive swift fox is small in stature and active mainly at night. Unusually for a fox, it is also bold and curious, and therefore easy to snare. In the past swift foxes were ruthlessly hunted for their highly prized fur.

THE SMALLEST OF NORTH AMERICA'S nine species of wild dog, the swift fox is about the size of a domestic cat. Swift foxes are generally nocturnal (active at night) and spend the day holed up in burrows, which they either dig for themselves or modify from the excavations of other prairie mammals. The burrows are fairly large and may have several entrances. During the spring and summer a burrow may contain as many as nine or 10 foxes, including a breeding pair and their offspring of the year. Occasionally a second adult female may also be present in the burrow. It takes the efforts of at least two adults to rear a litter of pups, which may number three to six, but the pair bond does not necessarily last from year to year.

Specialized Diet

A typical family will occupy a home range of about 12 square miles (31 sq. km), which is unusually large for a fox and reflects the species' more specialized food requirements. While most other foxes will eat almost anything, swift foxes are rather choosy about what they consume. Their preferred prey consists of gophers, pikas, and rabbits, although they will eat other animals and even grass and berries if there is no alternative. Swift foxes do particularly well in places where prey animals are plentiful, and their impressive acceleration is invaluable in catching the fleet-footed creatures they pursue. Over even terrain swift foxes can easily reach speeds of 30 miles per hour (48 km/h).

Swift foxes once roamed all over the central plains of North America, from Texas in the south to Saskatchewan and Alberta in the north. Today, however, the animals occupy a

SEE ALSO Coyote 2:58; Fox, Fennec 2:74; Gopher, Northern Pocket 7:26; Pika, American 8:98

mere 10 percent of that area, living in small, scattered populations with larger numbers at the center of their distributional range in Colorado and Wyoming. The relentless spread of agriculture across the prairies ruined much of the habitat of the swift fox. Plowing destroyed their burrows and those of their prey, and the planting of crops has changed the nature of the prairies forever.

Mistaken Identity

During the mid- to late 19th century there was a vigorous effort, supported by the United States government, to eradicate wolves and coyotes from the entire continent. Although swift foxes were not considered to be vermin, they could not be prevented from eating the poisoned baits put out to kill coyotes. Another problem was that they were (and still are) often mistaken for young coyotes, and many have been shot as a result of misidentification.

Unusually for foxes, the swift fox is bold and curious and therefore relatively easy to snare, shoot, and poison. Moreover, swift fox fur could fetch a good price, so there was every reason for the killing to continue. In the United States the foxes were wiped out of all but the southern part of their range by 1920. However, in the mid-20th century the species began to recover, spreading north once more into Wyoming, Nebraska, Oklahoma, Montana, and the Dakotas. But north of the border there was no such recovery, and by 1978 there were no swift foxes left in Canada.

It has taken an expensive and long-running program of reintroduction to restore a small population of swift foxes to southern Alberta and Saskatchewan. The northern populations are different enough from those in the south to be considered a separate subspecies, known as *Vulpes velox hebes*. They are darker than the southern foxes and have a broader muzzle.

⬅ *For nearly a century the diminutive swift fox suffered persecution through mistaken identity and trapping for its valuable fur.*

Common name Arctic fox

Scientific name Vulpes (Alopex) lagopus

Family Canidae

Order Carnivora

Size Length head/body: 18–27 in (46–68 cm); tail length: 12 in (30 cm); height at shoulder: 11 in (28 cm)

Weight 3–20 lb (1.4–9 kg)

Key features Stout-looking fox with short legs, long, bushy tail, small, rounded ears, and a thick, woolly coat; fur pure white in winter in high arctic animals; fur extends to soles of feet

Habits Social; sometimes migratory; active at any time of day; does not hibernate

Breeding Litters of 6–12 (occasionally as many as 25) pups born in early summer after gestation period of 49–57 days. Weaned at 2–4 weeks; sexually mature at 10 months. May live up to 16 years in captivity, many fewer in the wild

Voice Barks, whines, screams, and hisses

Diet Mainly carnivorous; prey includes seals, rodents (especially lemmings), seabirds, fish, invertebrates such as crabs, mollusks, and insects, and carrion; scavenges from kills made by other arctic predators; occasionally plant material

Habitat Arctic and northern alpine tundra, boreal forest, ice cap, and even sea ice

Distribution Arctic regions of Canada, Alaska, Greenland, Iceland, Finland, Sweden, Norway, and Russia

Status Population: abundant. Generally common, although range and population size have declined recently. Protected in Norway, Sweden, and Finland; hunted for fur and as vermin elsewhere

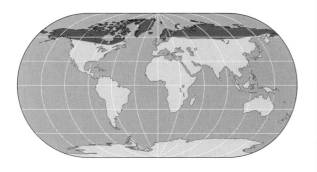

Arctic Fox

Vulpes (Alopex) lagopus

The Arctic fox has a number of adaptations in order to survive in extremely cold conditions. Nevertheless, life for the species can be very difficult, with many deprivations to endure.

As ITS NAME IMPLIES, THE RANGE of the hardy Arctic fox extends well beyond the Arctic Circle and farther north than any other member of the dog family. Arctic foxes have been recorded at latitudes as high as 88°N, only 150 miles (240 km) from the North Pole itself. But the foxes are only visitors to these frozen wastelands, and normally live farther south, especially in areas of coastal tundra in Canada, Greenland, Iceland, and northern Europe.

The southern edge of the Arctic fox's geographical range seems to be where the northern range of the red fox ends. Red foxes can make a living almost anywhere there is enough food to support them, but they are defeated by extreme cold. The Arctic fox here comes into its own, being able to tolerate temperatures that sometimes plummet to -58°F (-50°C). Captive individuals have been able to survive at -112°F (-80°C) under experimental conditions. Few other animals can tolerate such extreme cold.

Cold Weather Design

Both red and Arctic foxes have basically the same body shape, but the Arctic fox has relatively shorter legs and ears and a smaller muzzle. The Arctic fox's more compact shape is designed to lose less heat than the red fox's long and lean frame, which is built for speed and agility. Only the tail of the Arctic fox is very long, which allows it to be used as a kind of blanket to cover the fox's face while it sleeps. The most important adaptation to the cold is the Arctic fox's luxuriant fur. Said to be the warmest fur in the animal kingdom, it is fine, long, and fluffy. It is also incredibly dense, and in winter it grows to be three times as deep as

There are two color varieties of Arctic fox, known as white and blue. However, the white variety is only white in the winter months of October through April. Over the summer the fur usually turns a grayish-brown. White-furred foxes dominate the populations in Canada. In Greenland about half the foxes are white in winter, but in Iceland almost all of them are blue. Blue foxes are actually a steely gray color, which is darker in summer than in winter.

In addition to fur and body shape the Arctic fox has made a number of physiological adaptations to the cold. The fleshy parts of its paws are well supplied with blood vessels. Here, an extensive network of fine capillaries brings warm blood to the feet and toes, helping prevent frostbite. After passing through the feet, the cooled blood travels back up the leg past numerous other vessels carrying warm blood from the heart. The returning blood is in this way rewarmed before it enters the rest of the body to avoid it causing a drop in the fox's core body temperature.

Conserving Energy

In times of abundant food fat is accumulated under the skin, providing both insulation against the cold (like the blubber on a seal) and a reserve of energy for when food is scarce. In winter almost half the Arctic fox's body weight is fat. In especially hard times, when an Arctic fox has not eaten for many days, it is able to slow down its metabolism to about half the usual rate to save energy. The fox then has to be much less active than normal: It may even lay up in a snow hole for a while, but it does not actually hibernate. It stays fully alert and can spring into life as soon as a feeding opportunity arises.

Snow holes provide temporary shelter for wandering foxes, but for breeding purposes the animals require something more substantial. Arctic foxes build extensive dens,

↑ An Arctic fox displaying pure white winter coloration. The fur of the Arctic fox is said to be the warmest of all animals: The hairs of the coat are hollow to provide extra insulation in subzero temperatures.

in summer. Like the hairs in a polar bear's coat, those of the Arctic fox are hollow. Each individual hair therefore contains air, which helps provide extra insulation. Fur even grows on the soles of the fox's feet, protecting them from the chill of ice and snow. They also help the fox get a better grip in slippery, icy conditions. These furry feet are the reason for the animal's scientific name of *lagopus*, which literally means "rabbit-footed."

often in the base of a cliff or in a mound of earth and stones. Some of these dens have been in more or less continuous use for hundreds of years by generations of foxes. A den typically has several entrances, usually between four and a dozen, but sometimes up to 100. Long-established dens become quite a feature of the landscape, with taller vegetation growing around the entrances compared with elsewhere on the tundra. That is because of the extra nutrients from fox droppings and waste food that encourage the plants to grow.

Slim Chance of Survival

Arctic foxes are social animals, but groups are quite small: typically one breeding pair and their young of the year, plus a helper female (one of the previous year's offspring). Adult foxes mate for life and it takes all their efforts to raise a litter in what can be difficult conditions, even in summer. Litters are large, sometimes over 20 pups, but usually six to 12. The assistance of the young helper female means that two adults can hunt while a third stays at the den to baby-sit. Even so, the chances of any one youngster living longer than a few months are low and many die long before their first birthday. If they survive until the fall, the young foxes disperse to make their own way in life.

During the winter some foxes remain near the breeding den (especially if food is plentiful), but others undertake some of the most extraordinary journeys known in the animal kingdom. Sometimes they travel hundreds of miles from land, far out over the frozen sea. Foxes are not averse to swimming where necessary and can travel many miles by hitching a ride on an ice floe. In the winter the only food for foxes is whatever they can scavenge from the kills of polar bears. Beggars cannot be choosers, and Arctic foxes will eat anything from rotten meat to feces. Farther south and in summer their menu is more varied and includes birds, berries, and small mammals. For many fox populations lemmings form the main diet and at times are staggeringly abundant. However, every few years the lemming population crashes, and the foxes starve or are forced to search for alternative food, sometimes venturing hundreds of miles outside their normal range and far south of the snow line.

⬅ Arctic fox pups at their den. Litters are large (anything up to 25 pups), and parents are often assisted in baby-sitting duties by a female helper. Even so, the chances of a pup's survival are low.

➡ A barking Arctic fox displays its short summer coat. Over the summer months of May through September the fur usually turns a grayish-brown color. The coat can be up to three times as dense in winter as in summer.

The Fox Fur Trade

Arctic foxes have been hunted for their fur for hundreds of years. They are trapped in snares or shot almost everywhere except Scandinavia, where the population is very small and threatened with extinction. At the height of the fur trade foxes were extensively farmed in places like Alaska. Blue fox fur is considered more valuable by the fur trade, and the blue foxes living in Alaska and on the Aleutian Islands are almost all descendants of animals that escaped from fur farms. A good blue pelt can fetch about $300; but fashions change, and the demand is not as great as it once was. White foxes are hunted, too, but their fur is less valuable—in fact, it is sometimes dyed blue-gray in order to fetch a better price.

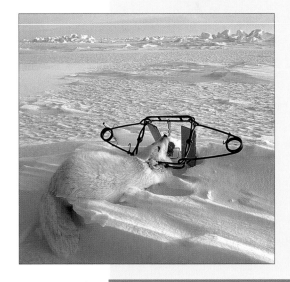

An Arctic fox caught in a trap. Foxes have been hunted for hundreds of years.

Common name Fennec fox

Scientific name *Vulpes (Fennecus) zerda*

Family Canidae

Order Carnivora

Size Length head/body: 14–16 in (35–41 cm); tail length: 7–12 in (18–30.5 cm); height at shoulder: 10 in (25 cm)

Weight 2.2–3.3 lb (1–1.5 kg)

Key features Small, dainty fox with huge, triangular ears and a long, bushy tail tipped with black; thick, pale, reddish-beige to white fur; soles of feet are also fur covered

Habits Social and territorial; nocturnal; lives in burrows

Breeding Two to 5 pups born in spring after gestation period of 50–52 days. Weaned at 9–10 weeks; sexually mature at 11 months. May live up to 14 years in captivity, probably about 8–10 in the wild

Voice Barks and whines; screams when fighting

Diet Small mammals, birds, reptiles, eggs, insects, and plant material

Habitat Desert and semidesert

Distribution Sahara Desert and North Africa, including parts of Morocco, Algeria, Tunisia, Mali, Niger, Libya, Chad, Egypt, and the Sudan

Status Population: widespread but uncommon; CITES II. A species in decline

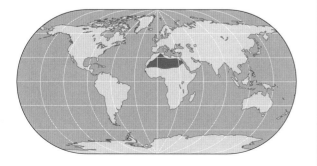

Fennec Fox *Vulpes (Fennecus) zerda*

The diminutive fennec fox is well adapted to life in its desert home. It is rarely seen, being active mainly at night, but hunters still pursue it for its luxurious fur.

THE WORLD'S LARGEST DESERT, the Sahara, is home to the smallest member of the dog family, the fennec fox. Fennecs are social and live in groups of up to about a dozen individuals, dominated by a single male. Dominance is established by fighting, sometimes to the death. Aggression is commonplace, and fights frequently break out over food. Members of the same group may share interconnected burrows, but nursing females are highly protective of their young and will not permit other foxes to come near. Fennecs form loyal breeding pairs, and the male diligently guards the area around the breeding burrow even though he is not allowed inside. He also hunts for the family and brings food to the burrow entrance for the female to collect.

Fennec burrows are surprisingly long for such a small animal and often extend more than 10 feet (3 m) into a sand dune. The foxes make the most of the scarce shade at the surface, and burrow entrances are usually found under rocks or at the base of sandy cliffs or dunes. The burrows stay relatively cool during the day and offer refuge from the sun.

Heat Resistant

Fennec foxes have a range of physical adaptations to the heat, including fully furred soles that insulate their paws from the hot ground. The fennec's tongue also turns up at the end to prevent drops of saliva dripping from the tip when it pants. Apart from enhancing the fox's sense of hearing, its huge ears act as heat conductors, radiating body heat into the air to help keep the animal cool. The fox's small size is another adaptation to the heat. Small animals have a relatively large surface area for their size, which means they lose excess body heat faster than large animals of a similar shape.

⬆ *The fennec fox's huge ears radiate heat into the air and help keep the animal cool. Even the soles of its feet are covered in fur to protect them against the bakingly hot ground.*

The furry feet of the fennec fox grip the sand better than the naked pads of other dogs, allowing the animal to run fast over loose sand. The feet also make highly effective digging tools, and the fox can burrow so fast that it appears to sink steadily into the sand before the observer's very eyes.

Nothing Wasted

In accordance with their digging habits, fennecs find much of their food by scrabbling in the sand. They also catch small animals by stalking and pouncing in a typically foxlike manner. Prey is killed with a quick bite to the neck and often swallowed whole. Any surplus food is rarely wasted. If a fox can avoid sharing its meal with others, it may cache (store) the leftovers by burying them. The fennec's teeth are sharp but rather weak and not adapted for slashing or tearing larger prey. Plant material forms a large part of the diet, and for some individuals this may be their only reliable source of water. Fennec foxes will drink from water holes if they have the opportunity, but they can get by without water for weeks at a time and may wander many miles from oases.

The unobtrusive, nocturnal lifestyle of the fennec fox means that it rarely comes into contact with humans; and unlike many other foxes, it is not considered a pest. However, fennecs are hunted widely for their luxurious fur and in some parts of Africa they are kept as pets. The species is not common anywhere and appears to be declining throughout its range. It has now been placed on Appendix II of CITES.

Common name Bat-eared fox

Scientific name *Otocyon megalotis*

Family	Canidae
Order	Carnivora
Size	Length head/body: 18–26 in (46–66 cm); tail length: 9–13.5 in (23–34 cm); height at shoulder: 12–16 in (30–40 cm)

Weight 6.6–11.6 lb (3–5.3 kg)

Key features Small, short-legged dog with thick, fuzzy-looking coat; fur is yellowish-brown but black on legs, feet, tail tip, and ears; small face with short muzzle; huge ears

Habits Social; generally active at night, but southern population is active during the day in winter

Breeding Litters of 2–6 pups born after gestation period of 60–70 days; births in September to November in southern Africa, all year round in the east. Weaned at 10 weeks; sexually mature at 9 months. May live up to 14 years in captivity, many fewer in the wild

Voice Soft whistling calls

Diet Mostly termites; also other invertebrates (such as dung beetles); some small mammals, birds, eggs, and plant material

Habitat Dry tropical grassland and scrub

Distribution East Africa: southern parts of Ethiopia and the Sudan; Somalia and Tanzania. Southern Africa: southern Angola, Zimbabwe, Botswana, Namibia, South Africa, and western Mozambique

Status Population: abundant. Secure, even expanding its range in places

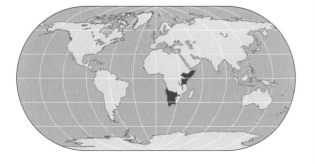

Bat-Eared Fox

Otocyon megalotis

The large ears and extra teeth of the bat-eared fox distinguish it from other members of the dog family and are adaptations to its mainly insectivorous diet, which may also include small lizards and mice.

THE BAT-EARED FOX IS UNIQUE IN several ways. In terms of outward appearance its huge ears mark it out from other dogs. It also has more teeth than any other carnivore, usually 48, compared with the 42 of most other dogs. The extra teeth are molars. Both ears and teeth are adaptations to the bat-eared fox's largely insectivorous diet. These unique features are enough for some scientists to classify the bat-eared fox in its own subfamily.

Termite Eaters

Bat-eared fox habitat is dictated by the availability of its main prey, the harvester termite. Harvester termites live in grazed grasslands with dry, sandy soils warmed by the sun. They emerge above ground to collect grass, which they take back to the colony. They are easy to catch—the fox simply collects them off the grass with its tongue. The other important insect prey is dung beetles, some of which can be the size of a golf ball. The foxes catch adult beetles on the surface and dig the grubs out of the ground. Dung beetle grubs

hatch in balls of dung that are collected and buried by their parents. The bat-eared fox uses its enormous ears to pinpoint the precise position of the grubs as they munch their way through the buried dung.

Both termites and beetles depend on the nibblings of large hooved animals to keep grass short and to produce large amounts of dung. Animals such as antelope, zebra, and domestic cattle help maintain the ideal conditions for the insects. If grazing stops, however, the grass grows long, the insects decline, and the foxes cannot find enough to eat, so they have to move on. In very dry areas, such as the Karroo Desert in South Africa, the foxes eat more fruit to compensate for the lack of drinking water.

It is largely thanks to grazing livestock that bat-eared foxes have recently expanded their range into Botswana and Mozambique. Elsewhere, however, the species has declined, often as a consequence of increased areas of land being taken up by farm crops. Although the foxes do not threaten sheep and cattle and are not generally considered pests, they are sometimes hunted for their fur. They are also occasionally harassed by domestic dogs and can

⤓ *Where the bat-eared fox lives is determined by its main food source of harvester termites. Recently it has even been able to expand its range into Botswana and Mozambique.*

catch rabies from them. Rabies is the main cause of death in many populations, with mini epidemics often wiping out more than a quarter of the foxes in reserves such as the Serengeti National Park in northern Tanzania.

Behavioral Variations

The behavior of bat-eared foxes varies in different parts of their range. In areas where termites are concentrated in clumps, but nevertheless abundant, the home ranges of many foxes overlap, and the animals ignore each other or interact amicably. Elsewhere they are aggressively intolerant, especially to other members of the same sex.

The breeding season varies in different parts of Africa, but almost always coincides with the rainy season, when insect food is at its most abundant. Bat-eared foxes forage alone, except in young families in which the cubs follow their parents to learn how to find food. Family groups are generally small, consisting of a breeding pair and their offspring. The young foxes are born in a large den with many entrances, but will be moved regularly to other dens in the parents' range to reduce the risk of predation. The youngsters are fully independent at 10 months old and leave their parents at about this age.

Common name African wild dog (African hunting dog, painted hunting dog)

Scientific name *Lycaon pictus*

Family   Canidae

Order   Carnivora

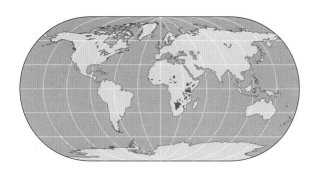

Size   Length head/body: 30–44 in (76–112 cm); tail length: 12–16 in (30–41 cm); height at shoulder: 24–31 in (61–78 cm)

Weight 37.5–80 lb (17–36 kg)

Key features Lean, long-legged dog with large ears and 4 toes on each foot (other dogs have 5 digits on front feet); fur is short, thin, and patterned with variable blotches and speckles of black, brown, yellow, and white; dark skin often shows through coat

Habits   Highly social; active by day; packs wander widely except when breeding

Breeding   Litters of up to 20 pups (usually 4–8) born at any time of year after gestation period of 79–80 days. Weaned at 11 weeks; sexually mature at 2 years. May live up to 17 years in captivity, 11 in the wild

Voice   Excited squeaks and twitters; also hoots and wails that carry long distances

Diet: Carnivorous, mostly taking hoofed mammals such as antelope

Habitat   Savanna grassland and open woodland

Distribution Africa south of the Sahara

Status   Population: probably fewer than 5,000 and declining; IUCN Endangered. Protected by law in most of its range

African Wild Dog

Lycaon pictus

African wild dogs are among the most social of animals. Their packs are model societies in which every member is taken care of from birth.

NO OTHER WILD DOG HAS SUCH a colorful and varied coat as the African wild dog, and few other animals appear to live in such close harmony as this unmistakable species. The members of a pack indulge in daily meeting ceremonies before going out hunting. They mingle excitedly, nuzzling each other and making squeaky, twittering sounds. Prey may be chased for up to an hour, but usually much less, before it is pulled down and killed. The dogs always share their kills amicably, and any elderly or injured dogs are given a share, even though they may have played no part in the hunt.

For most of the year the dogs are nomadic, traveling widely within a range that may be as large as 1,500 square miles (4,000 sq. km). The ranges of neighboring packs overlap extensively, but there is no marking of boundaries or other territorial behavior. Dogs from different packs may meet from time to time, especially where there is a lot of prey, but aggression is rare.

Pups Cared for by Whole Pack

During the breeding season the pack's range is much smaller, often under 80 square miles (200 sq. km). Even the nonbreeding animals stay close to the breeding den, usually an old aardvark hole. The pups are cared for by all members of the pack, who take turns baby-sitting while the rest go hunting. At three weeks, when the pups are ready to begin weaning, the adults regurgitate meat for them. When they are old enough to follow the hunt, they are given priority at the kill, even ahead of the dominant male and female. Once the young dogs are able to fend for themselves (at about four months), females will begin to leave in

search of another pack or to start their own. African wild dogs are unique among social carnivores, since it is the females, not the males, that disperse and compete for breeding rights. Males are more likely to stay and may spend their whole lives in one pack.

Hierarchy

Wild dog packs contain more males than females, and they are usually related to each other. Both sexes have their own hierarchy, and the dominant pair (the "top dogs") are often the only ones to breed. Females can become aggressive in the fight for dominance; and if a second female should succeed in having a litter, the dominant female will sometimes try to steal the pups, claiming them as her own. The contests can result in a distressing tug-of-war, which the cubs

⊕ African wild dogs are unique among social carnivores, since it is the young females that compete for breeding rights. They are also the ones that leave their birth pack when they reach maturity.

rarely survive. Such brutality is not the norm, however, and as long as the lead female is unchallenged, the pack is a model of teamwork and unselfish behavior.

At one time hunting dogs could be found throughout Africa south of the Sahara and also in Egypt. Today their distribution is patchy, with no more than about 5,000 animals left in the whole of Africa. The decline is largely due to loss of suitable habitats, which have been taken over for agricultural use. Once these large areas start to be farmed, the dogs are a potential danger to livestock and are often killed by farmers. Farm animals also bring disease, and hunting-dog populations have suffered badly from rabies and canine distemper transmitted by domestic dogs.

Common name Dingo

Scientific name *Canis dingo (C. lupus dingo)*

Family	Canidae
Order	Carnivora
Size	Length head/body: 34–48 in (86–122 cm); tail length: 10–15 in (26–38 cm); height at shoulder: 17–25 in (44–63 cm)

Weight 22–53 lb (10–24 kg)

Key features Large robust-looking dog; sandy fur with pale markings on feet, chest, muzzle, and tail tip; long muzzle and pricked ears; bushy tail

Habits Lives in packs of up to 12, defending common territory; hunts alone or in packs

Breeding One to 10 (average 5) pups born in underground den during winter after gestation period of 63 days. Weaned at 3 months; sexually mature at 2 years. May live a little over 14 years in captivity, up to 14 in the wild

Voice Typical doglike bark, whines, yelps, and howls

Diet Varies according to prey available; anything from kangaroos and rabbits to insects and carrion

Habitat Diverse; hot deserts, tropical and temperate forests, mountains, scrub, and ranch land

Distribution Australia, New Guinea, Indochina, Indonesia, Borneo, and Philippines

Status Population: abundant. Declining in numbers, but not included in any conservation programs because most countries do not protect introduced or alien species

Dingo

Canis dingo

Although thought of as an Australian animal, the dingo is not in fact a native, but an intelligent and adaptable immigrant, which soon became the country's top predator.

SOME ZOOLOGISTS BELIEVE THAT the dingo is descended from a kind of Asian wolf; others say its ancestor is an early form of the domestic dog. There is probably truth in both suggestions, since the first domestic dogs were little more than tame wolves. What is almost certain, however, is that the first dogs to arrive in Australia about 4,000 years ago had some help getting there. This suggests that they were at least partially domesticated. Aboriginal people used dingoes to hunt large animals and perhaps for companionship, but these animals were doubtless still a little wild at heart.

Clever Newcomer

Dingoes are smart, hardy, and adaptable animals, and in a very short time they spread throughout Australia. They can travel quite large distances in search of food, but they are not fussy about what they eat and can survive happily in a wide variety of environments. In a short time they became the top predator in Australia. Their only native competitor was the marsupial wolf, or thylacine (also known as the Tasmanian tiger), which sadly proved no match for the fast, intelligent newcomer. The thylacine disappeared from mainland Australia within 2,000 years of the dingo's arrival. From then on the only remaining thylacine population was on the island of Tasmania. There are no dingoes in Tasmania, so dingoes cannot be blamed for the thylacine's eventual extinction in the 1930s.

Dingoes are sociable and live in packs, although individuals often wander alone for days at a time. Each animal is capable of hunting small prey by itself, but large prey animals require teamwork to catch and kill. When natural prey are in short supply, dingoes

often resort to hunting livestock. The size of a dingo pack's territory depends largely on the quality of the habitat, especially the availability of water and prey. The territory is maintained by scent marking and howling sessions.

Breeding happens just once a year, and caring for the young is a team effort. In stable packs young adults help the more dominant animals rear litters of pups by bringing in food and by baby-sitting. Quite often only one female will be allowed to breed, thus ensuring that her litter has the best possible chance of survival. The other females, usually the elder daughters of the dominant female, tend to remain faithful to the pack in which they were born, waiting for the chance to breed one day themselves. Young males are more likely to move on and may wander for many months before finding a mate and a place to settle.

Threats for the Future

Dingoes were regarded as vermin that posed a danger to sheep and lambs. As a result, they were poisoned and shot in large numbers. However, killing the dominant female in a pack allows several subdominant animals to breed instead, and more dingoes than usual are born!

Dingoes are not exclusively Australian. Dingolike dogs have colonized many other parts of the world in the past, and some populations survive in parts of Southeast Asia. However, virtually all dingo populations are facing an uncertain future owing to changes in their habitats, persecution by humans, and hybridization with domestic dogs. In years to come there may still be dogs living wild in Australia and other places, but they will no longer be purebred dingoes. The nonnative status of dingoes throughout their range means they do not receive protection, despite having been an established part of the environment for thousands of years.

⊝ *A male dingo digs out a rabbit from its warren. Once regarded as useful hunting animals, dingoes are now often treated as vermin.*

The Bear Family

Bears share the same ancestors as dogs, but they are also distantly related to cats, otters, and other members of the order Carnivora. Bears appear to have evolved in Asia, but they soon colonized the Americas, Europe, and Africa. The earliest bearlike animal was small, probably weighing well under 44 pounds (20 kg). It had a long tail and a relatively small skull with sharp teeth designed for shearing meat. This so-called "dawn bear" is known only from fossils about 20 million years old. Fossils from more recent times tell the story of the bear family's evolution from small meat-eaters to the much larger omnivorous animals we know today. As the typical bear body got bigger and heavier, the tail all but disappeared, and the head became larger. The enlarged skull was necessary in order to accommodate the huge jaw muscles needed to grind up tough vegetable food. The teeth changed too. The pointed and shearing teeth became squarer and flatter, adapted for chewing and grinding rather than cutting.

What Is a Bear?

Bears are large, heavy-bodied mammals with thick, shaggy fur and a very short tail. They have a large head with small, round ears, small eyes, and powerful jaws with big teeth. They generally walk on four legs, although most can walk a short distance on two. Bears are surprisingly agile for their size, and the majority can climb well. Most bears can swim, and one, the polar bear, is equally at home in water and on land. Its paws are paddle shaped, and its toes are partially webbed.

All bears are large animals, and even the smallest members of the smallest species (the Malaysian sun bear) still exceed 40 inches (100 cm) in length and weigh at least 60 pounds (27 kg). The largest species is the polar bear, adult males of which reach nearly 9 feet (2.7 m) long and weigh in at a massive 1,750 pounds (800 kg). This makes them the world's largest land-dwelling predators. Male grizzly bears can grow to a similar size.

Lifestyle

As a general rule, bears are omnivorous or vegetarian. Only the polar bear is fully carnivorous, with seals forming the bulk of its diet. However, even this species may eat plant material during the summer when the sea ice melts and it is forced to come onto land. The other species eat fruit, leaves and shoots, honey, small animals, eggs, and fish. Bears have a reputation for being greedy, and indeed, many seem to spend most of their waking hours eating. But because they have evolved from meat-eating ancestors, bears do not have a fully efficient gut for digesting plant material. Much of what they eat passes straight through their bodies without being properly digested. As a result, they have to eat a great deal to sustain themselves.

Bear courtship is usually brief, and rearing the offspring is the sole responsibility of the mother. Pregnancies are often surprisingly long owing to a variable period of delayed implantation, during which the newly formed embryos do not develop, but simply wait in the uterus until the mother bear has reached peak condition. The pregnancy is only allowed to proceed if the female is fit enough to develop and care for the young. Bear cubs are born very small and need an extended period of care, sometimes several years.

Apart from mothers with cubs and courting pairs, bears live alone. However, they are not necessarily

---

Family Ursidae: 5 genera, 8 species

Tremarctos 1 species, Andean or spectacled bear (*T. ornatus*)

Ailuropoda 1 species, giant panda (*A. melanoleuca*)

Ursus 4 species, American black bear (*U. americanus*); brown/grizzly bear (*U. arctos*); polar bear (*U. maritimus*); Asian black bear (*U. thibetanus*)

Melursus 1 species, sloth bear (*M. ursinus*)

Helarctos 1 species, sun bear (*H. malayanus*)

⬅ *A snarling Alaskan brown (or grizzly) bear. Bears look fierce, but attacks on humans are rare and usually involve some kind of provocation.*

⬇ *The four species of smaller, lesser-known bears: an Asian black bear feeds on carrion (1); an Andean (spectacled) bear climbs a tree in search of fruit (2); a sun bear catches termites on its tongue (3); and a sloth bear forages for insects (4).*

territorial, and their home ranges (which can be huge) usually overlap with those of other individuals. Scent marks and other signs keep the bears informed of their neighbors' movements and help avoid unexpected meetings. Bears are aggressive, especially mothers with cubs and males competing for dominance. Young males are particularly vulnerable to attack by older males, since their seniors try to rid the area of rivals. In places where the bear population density is very high, there is usually a dominance hierarchy, which helps keep the peace when several individuals gather together, for example, around a shared food source.

Most bears spend a considerable amount of time in dens, which can be caves, hollow trees, or chambers dug in the earth or snow. Alternatively, they can simply be sheltered spaces amid dense vegetation. Dens are most important for those species that live in seasonal zones

(away from the tropics). Bears living in such climates are known to suffer from serious food shortages at certain times of year. In order to get around the problem, they put on as much weight as they can during the summer and fall, then sleep for much of the winter in a secure den, living off their fat reserves.

Common name Polar bear

Scientific name *Ursus maritimus*

Family	Ursidae
Order	Carnivora
Size	Length head/body: 6.6–8.2 ft (2–2.5 m); tail length: 3–5 in (7–13 cm); height at shoulder: up to 5.2 ft (1.6 m)

Weight Male 660–1,760 lb (300–800 kg); female 330–660 lb (50–300 kg)

Key features	Huge bear with thick, off-white coat; head relatively small; feet large and furry
Habits	Solitary; migratory and partially nomadic; pregnant females hibernate in winter; excellent swimmer
Breeding	Litters of 1–4 tiny cubs born in midwinter after gestation period of 195–265 days (includes variable period of delayed implantation). Weaned from 6 months; sexually mature at 5–6 years. May live up to 45 years in captivity, 30 in the wild
Voice	Grunts and growls
Diet	Carnivorous: mainly seals but occasionally other animals such as reindeer; also fish, seabirds, carrion, and plant material in summer
Habitat	Sea ice, ice cap, and tundra; equally at home in water and on land
Distribution	Arctic Circle; parts of Canada, Alaska, Russia, Scandinavia, and Greenland
Status	Population: 20,000–30,000; IUCN Lower Risk: conservation dependent; CITES II. Main threat is from human exploitation of Arctic habitats

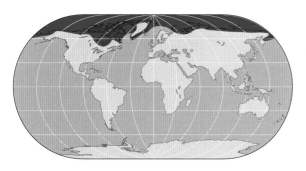

Polar Bear

Ursus maritimus

The polar bear is the world's largest land carnivore and is superbly adapted to life in one of the harshest regions on earth.

POLAR BEARS AND BROWN BEARS are more closely related than their appearance and different lifestyles suggest. Until about 100,000 years ago they were the same species, and even today individuals in captivity are able to interbreed. The special features that allow polar bears to survive life in and out of the water in one of the bleakest, most inhospitable parts of the world are all fairly recent adaptations, providing a good example of how evolution can proceed quickly under extreme conditions.

Cold Weather Protection

The most striking polar bear characteristic is, of course, its color. But there is more to the coat than meets the eye. Not only are the hairs very long, trapping a deep layer of warm air against the skin, but (under a microscope) the individual hairs can be seen to be hollow. Each has air spaces running along its length, which help make the coat extra warm because air trapped inside the hairs improves the insulation effect. It is the hollowness of the hairs and the lack of pigment that makes the fur appear white. The dense coat is also surprisingly light. Late in the season, before the fur is molted, it begins to look rather yellow, owing to a combination of accumulated dirt and the oxidizing effect of sunlight. Zoo polar bears sometimes get algae from their pool into the coat hairs, turning them temporarily green, but this does not happen in the wild!

The other obvious feature of polar bears is their size. Fully grown males are the world's largest terrestrial predators, measuring about 8 feet (2.5 m) long on all fours and weighing as much as 10 large men. Females are less than half this size, but still number among the world's most powerful animals. Large body size

is another adaptation to the cold, because larger animals are more efficient at preventing loss of body heat. Being big also allows polar bears to tackle large prey—for much of the year seals are the only other animals around, and a polar bear can scoop one out of the water using just a single paw. Another special adaptation is the huge furry feet, which help spread the polar bear's weight so effectively that a bear weighing half a ton (508 kg) can walk carefully across ice too thin to support a human. The soles are also furry, protecting the pads from frostbite and giving the bear extra grip on the ice: They also help reduce the tendency to sink into soft snow. The bears are

⊕ Polar bears test their strength in bouts of play wrestling. Fully grown males are the world's largest terrestrial predators and can weigh as much as 10 large men.

nimble for their size and can gallop at speeds of up to 30 miles per hour (50 km/h) for relatively short periods.

Long-Distance Traveler

Polar bears have never actually been recorded at the North Pole. Here the sea ice is thick and continuous, with no access to open water for the bears or for the seals on which they feed. However, they do occur almost everywhere else within the Arctic Circle, concentrating their activity around the thin, cracked edges of the pack ice where seals haul out. In winter, when the sea ice reaches its maximum extent, the bears venture as far south as Newfoundland, southern Greenland, and the Bering Sea.

Polar bears wander widely, but they are not true nomads as was once believed. Recent studies show that bears from different parts of the Arctic form distinct populations, with individual bears using ranges of up to 200,000 square miles (500,000 sq. km) over the course of a few years. There is a resident population of polar bears around the Hudson and James Bays,

⬆ *A female polar bear with her cubs. Polar bear cubs stay with their mother for about two and a half years, only leaving when she is ready to breed again.*

members of which do not need to travel so far. They spend their summers on land, venturing up to 120 miles (200 km) inland, and move out onto the vast expanse of ice when the bays freeze over in winter.

Smash and Grab

Ringed seals are the most important prey species, and polar bears show considerable flexibility in the techniques used to hunt them. In late spring female ringed seals give birth to their young in well-hidden dens. The dens have openings to the sea below but are invisible from above, being roofed over with snow. However, polar bears have an acute sense of smell and can detect the pups lying quietly below. They break into the den using brute force, rearing up on their hind legs and

Delayed Implantation

Most polar bears are solitary and wander over vast areas. Males and females rarely meet, so they are ready to mate whenever the opportunity occurs between March and June. Whatever the time of mating, the cubs are nearly always born in midwinter. It is the best time of year for births because it allows the maximum period for growth and development after the babies have left the den. A polar bear's pregnancy can therefore be anything from six and a half to almost nine months. Soon after fertilization of the mother's eggs the tiny embryos go into a state of suspended animation. It is the fact that the embryos do not begin to develop immediately that makes the variable gestation period possible. Pregnancy and rearing cubs over the winter put a huge strain on the female's body and can be fatal if she is not in good health. Delaying the development of the embryos until the female has put on enough weight to survive the pregnancy and provide milk for the cubs through the winter guards against starvation of the entire family. If the female is not in top condition by the late fall, the embryos are spontaneously aborted.

pounding the roof with their front feet. They then seize the seal pup inside. Hunting adult seals, on the other hand, is all about stealth and patience. Bears wait silently by a breathing hole for a seal to emerge, then grab it and heave the animal onto the ice. Sometimes the bears sneak up on a seal resting on the ice, using snow ridges and ice blocks as cover. They creep forward in a low crouch, keeping still every time the seal looks around. Not every hunt is successful, but the bears often kill enough to feed not only themselves but an entourage of scavenging Arctic foxes as well.

Varied Diet

Individual bears have distinctly different hunting techniques, which they develop according to their own experience. Other items that may appear on the polar bear's menu include harp and bearded seals, young beluga whales, walrus, reindeer, fish, seabirds, dead animals, and occasionally plant material. Bears arriving on land in the summer may spend hours browsing on leaves and berries, which, although not especially nutritious, contain some vitamins and minerals otherwise completely lacking in the bear's diet. For many bears summer is a time of hunger because the lack of sea ice means they cannot hunt seals. The Hudson Bay bears may go for months without eating, living only on their fat reserves and staying as inactive as possible to save energy and to avoid overheating in the weak sunshine.

Breeding Dens

Most polar bears remain active throughout the winter, only seeking shelter in temporary snow holes during the worst storms. They do not normally need to hibernate because there is no shortage of food at this time of year. Pregnant females, however, build substantial dens in which to spend the winter. The dens, which are dug into a bank of snow, usually consist of a tunnel up to 10 feet (3 m) long and a large oval chamber. Some are rather more elaborate and may have several interconnected rooms. The female sleeps in the den throughout the winter,

The Sea Bear

The polar bear could just as correctly be called the sea bear (indeed, its scientific name means precisely that). It is a superb swimmer and is just as comfortable in the icy water of the Arctic Ocean as on land or pack ice. Polar bears can float effortlessly in seawater and do not sink even when dead. The hollow hairs in their coat are much more buoyant than normal fur. The fur is also slightly greasy and repels water. After a swim the bear only needs one quick shake to remove most of the moisture from its coat, so there is little danger of ice forming in the fur. The toes of the bear's enormous paddle-shaped feet are slightly webbed, making them more effective for swimming. The bear's neck is long, and it swims with its head held high above the water so that it has a good view over the waves.

Polar bears can swim for hours, using a steady dog paddle. They have even been known to swim up to 40 miles (65 km) across open water. They can dive under ice and climb out through seal breathing holes or leap 7 feet (2 m) onto ice cliffs. Hitching a ride on a passing ice floe is a favorite way of getting around, and the bears seem quite happy to plunge in and out of the cold water dozens of times a day.

⊙ *Polar bears are excellent swimmers and can paddle for hours at a time.*

during which time the cubs are born. They are very small and need protecting from the harsh climate for the first few months of life. The newborn young make their own way to their mother's teats, and she suckles them without appearing to wake up. This long sleep is not true hibernation because although the female's heart rate and breathing slow down, her body temperature only drops by a few degrees. As a result, the den remains cozy, and she can wake up quickly if need be. By the time spring comes, the cubs have increased in weight from

just over 1 pound (500 g) to between 25 and
30 pounds (11 and 14 kg) apiece. The mother
is half-starved, having used up most of her fat
to produce milk. Her first priority is to find
food, but that is not easy with up to three lively
cubs romping by her side.

Bear Attacks

Polar bears are aggressive. They can and do kill
humans; but since little of their range is
populated, the number of fatalities is low.
People who live and work within the polar
bear's range are generally well informed when
it comes to bears, and visitors are given plenty
of advice on how to avoid danger. Bear attacks
are most frequent in the Hudson Bay area,
especially around the town of Churchill, where
several people have been attacked in the last 40
years. The bears pass by the town on their
regular migrations and are attracted to the
municipal waste dumps where they are liable to
attack anyone who disturbs them.

⊖ *Polar bears wander widely, with individuals using
ranges of up to 200,000 square miles (500,000 sq. km)
over the course of a few years.*

Polar Bears and Humans

Polar bears have been known to the Inuit people from
the time they settled in the North American Arctic
about 4,000 years ago. The bears figure prominently in
native folklore and spirituality. They were traditionally
hunted for meat, fur, and other body parts. More
recently polar bears were also hunted commercially, but
the practice ceased in 1976 as the result of an
agreement between the five "Polar Bear Nations"—the
United States, Canada, Norway, Russia, and Denmark.
Conservation laws now include controls on commercial
hunting: Most of the bears hunted today are killed as
part of the traditional Inuit hunt. However, hunting is
not the only threat, and polar bears currently face
problems associated with pollution and the exploitation
of the Arctic for mining and oil extraction.

Common name American black bear

Scientific name *Ursus americanus*

Family	Ursidae
Order	Carnivora
Size	Length head/body: 4.9–5.9 ft (1.5–1.8 m); tail length: 4.5 in (12 cm); height at shoulder: up to 36 in (91 cm)
	Weight Male 250–600 lb (113–272 kg); female 200–310 lb (91–141 kg)
Key features	Large bear with thick, but not shaggy coat; fur can be variety of colors, but usually brown or black; muzzle less furry than rest of face
Habits	Solitary; most active at night; swims and climbs well; hibernates over winter
Breeding	Litters of 1–5 (usually 2 or 3) cubs born after gestation period of 220 days (including about 150 days delayed implantation). Weaned at 6–8 months; females sexually mature at 4–5 years, males at 5–6 years. May live up to 31 years in captivity, 26 in the wild
Voice	Various grunts, rumbling growls, and woofing sounds; cubs give high-pitched howls
Diet	Mostly plant material, including fruit, nuts, grass, bark, and roots; fish; invertebrates such as insects and their larvae and worms; also honey, other mammals, and carrion
Habitat	Forest and scrub; occasionally open spaces
Distribution	Canada, Alaska, and U.S. south to Mexico
Status	Population: 400,000–500,000; CITES II. Still common, but population now reduced due to hunting, persecution, and habitat loss

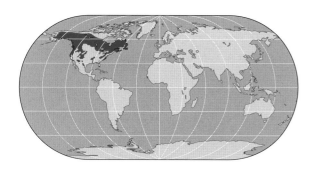

American Black Bear

Ursus americanus

Think of the American black bear, and the image of the cartoon character "Yogi Bear" may well come to mind. In fact, the black bear is very similar to the adaptable and opportunistic forager portrayed in the TV show.

THE AMERICAN BLACK BEAR HAS always been widespread and remains common over much of its huge geographical range. It is a typical bear, and its enterprising and opportunistic behavior has made it the inspiration for myths, folk tales and modern stories, films, and cartoons. Even so, the details of its biology have only recently become well understood. Before the 1960s and 1970s zoologists lacked the necessary skills and technology to make safe, nondisruptive, long-term observations of these shy but powerful animals in the wild. Since that time live trapping, radio tracking, and other up-to-date techniques have provided much information about the bear's daily life and behavior patterns.

Color Variations

American black bears can be a variety of colors ranging from white to black and including reddish and chocolate brown, bluish-black, and dark blond. However, dark-brown or black individuals are by far the most common. There are geographical trends in color variation, with most nonblack bears occurring in the southwest in California and Mexico. The white form (not to be confused with the polar bear, which is another species entirely) is rare, but most white bears come from the Pacific coast of southwestern Canada.

Black bears are not particularly aggressive toward people; but like all large animals, they can be unpredictable and dangerous, especially if they are injured, frightened, or provoked. Black bears generally avoid confrontations with humans, but their opportunistic foraging habits can bring them very close to areas of human

ⓤ *An adult black bear rests on a fallen log. Black bear habitat is usually forest or scrubland, but bears will occasionally venture into open spaces and even the fringes of towns.*

activity and thus into potentially tragic situations. Fatal black bear attacks are rare, but they always receive high-profile publicity.

Black bears normally live alone, except for courting pairs, mothers with cubs, and occasional gatherings around a plentiful food resource, such as a waste dump. Each has a separate territory; but home ranges can overlap, so that in areas of prime habitat, such as Washington State's Long Island and parts of California, they can live at densities of two or three bears per square mile (about one per sq. km). Male bears are more territorial than females, and the overlaps between their ranges are small or nonexistent. However, the size and shape of a male's home range are usually determined by the ranges of the local females—the male occupies a space that gives him access to as many potential mates as possible.

While the bears in a local area usually keep to themselves as much as possible, there is often a loosely structured social hierarchy, which comes into play when the bears meet.

① Coat color ranges from black to white, depending on geographical location. Bears from southeastern Alaska (above) have a bluish-gray coloration.

"Smarter than the Average Bear"

So goes the catchphrase of the famous cartoon character Yogi Bear, and it is a true description of the cleverness of black bears. The species will eat just about anything it can lay its paws on; but like people, black bears are especially partial to high-energy foods and those with a high fat and protein content. Yogi Bear and his sidekick Booboo are fictional of course, but their endless quest for unguarded picnic hampers is not far short of reality. National parks throughout the black bear's range have strict rules on the safe storage and disposal of food. Backpackers are advised never to keep food in their tents to reduce the risk of nighttime raids by clever bears who have learned where to get an easy meal. Official campgrounds usually provide lockable metal boxes in which food can be kept out of reach. Wilderness campers are advised to use hanging larders, since even smart bears find them difficult to break into. Park bears have become used to people, cars, and roads, and are intelligent enough to recognize sealed soft drink cans and other unnatural-looking objects as food.

A picnic hamper is never safe with Yogi and Booboo around!

For example, males competing for a female will size each other up with aggressive posturing, rearing up on two legs, and wrestling with one another. An inferior bear will back down, while two closely matched bears may come to serious blows. The bear that emerges victorious from the bout will probably retain his dominance next time the two meet, so avoiding the need for more violence.

Moving In

Good black bear country is rugged, with plenty of tree cover. Historically black bears were probably discouraged from venturing far onto the Canadian tundra at the north of their range by the presence of brown/grizzly bears. Grizzlies not only present stiff competition for food and shelter, but they will occasionally kill small black bears. However, where the tundra grizzlies have declined (due to hunting and persecution), it seems that the black bear is only too happy to move into the vacated territory to forage. One of the most

⊙ *A cinnamon-colored mother (sow) with her cubs. Up to five cubs are born in January or February. They stay in their underground den, suckling from their mother, until quite late in the spring.*

⊙ *The opportunistic foraging habits of bears can often bring them into close contact with humans, sometimes with tragic consequences. Here, an American black bear scavenges at a waste dump in Canada.*

important requirements of bear country is enough suitable hibernation sites. Black bears hibernate because there is not enough food available during the winter to sustain them in normal activity. Many of the bear's natural food sources are highly seasonal, with fruit, berries, and nuts all peaking in late summer.

During this time of plenty the bears gorge themselves, becoming fat and lethargic. By mid-fall, when most of the food is gone, they stop eating and seek out a secure den in which to spend the winter. It might be a cave, a hollowed-out log, or the space under a fallen tree. Some dens are used every year by the same or different individuals.

Winter Slumber

Once asleep, the black bear's core body temperature drops four to seven degrees to between 93.2 and 87.8°F (34 and 31°C). Its breathing and heart rate slow right down until its metabolism is just ticking over using the bare minimum of energy. The bear will stay in that torpid state as long as the cold weather lasts, but will rouse during short periods of warm weather, sometimes even emerging from the den for a day or two. Bears that live in the north hibernate for longer than those in the south, and the winter sleep can last anything from 75 to 130 days. When they emerge from

their den, the bears will selectively forage for the richest food in order to regain the weight they lost over the winter months of hibernation.

Females that mated the previous summer may give birth while they hibernate. Like many other carnivores, American black bear embryos undergo a period of suspended development soon after they are conceived. They do not implant into the mother's uterus until her body is in prime condition and she has put on enough weight to be able to support herself and her developing cubs during the winter. The mother bear may not get the chance to eat again until quite late in the spring when the cubs will be two or three months old.

The cubs are born in January or February and are virtually naked when they first appear. They weigh only 8 ounces (230 g). They suckle from their sleeping mother's teats, putting on weight and becoming livelier almost by the day. By the time spring arrives and the family emerges from the den, the cubs are fully furred bundles of energy. They continue to suckle for a further four to six months and are gradually weaned onto solid food, which their mother teaches them to find. The young bears will spend the whole summer and the following winter with their mother. They will usually disperse at about 18 months of age, leaving her free to have another family.

Common name Brown bear (grizzly bear, big brown bear)

Scientific name *Ursus arctos*

Family   Ursidae

Order   Carnivora

Size   Length head/body: 5.5–9.3 ft (1.7–2.8 m); tail length: 2.5–8 in (6–20 cm); height at shoulder: 35–60 in (90–150 cm). Male bigger than female

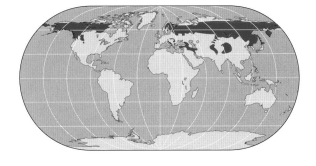

Weight 132–1,750 lb (60–800 kg)

Key features Medium to large bear with shaggy, light-brown to black fur, often grizzled (grayish) on back and shoulders; narrow snout; broad face

Habits   Solitary; nonterritorial; hibernates over winter

Breeding   Litters of 1–4 (usually 2) cubs born January–March after gestation period of 180–266 days. Weaned at 5 months; sexually mature at 4–6 years. May live up to 40 years in captivity, 25 in the wild

Voice   Various grunts and growls

Diet   Mostly plant material, including grass, roots, and fungi; also invertebrates such as worms and insects and their larvae; fish and carrion

Habitat   Varied; tundra, open plains, alpine grassland, forests, and wooded areas

Distribution Western Canada, Alaska, and northwestern U.S.; northern Asia south of Arctic Circle; Scandinavia, eastern Europe, and Middle East; Pyrenees, Alps, and Abruzzi Mountains

Status   Population: 220,000; CITES I (several Eurasian subspecies); CITES II (North American subspecies). Declining, but now more stable

Brown/Grizzly Bear

Ursus arctos

This highly successful and widespread bear ranges widely across the Northern Hemisphere. The largest brown bears occur in the United States and are often referred to as grizzly bears.

AMONG THE WORLD'S MOST FEARED and admired carnivores, the brown bear (known as the grizzly bear in parts of North America) is also one of the largest and most prevalent. At its most widespread its range covered most of North America, Europe, and Asia. It still occurs widely in all three continents; but its distribution is now more patchy, and some smaller populations are seriously threatened with extinction. Because of its size and strength the brown bear has been a feared neighbor for country people over many centuries.

Regional Variations

Brown bears from different geographical areas vary greatly in appearance and behavior. Most are some shade of brown, but off-white and almost black individuals are known. The largest bears are found on the Pacific coast of Alaska, specifically on Kodiak and Admiralty Islands. Males here reach almost 1,750 pounds (800 kg) in weight, rivaling the largest polar bears in size.

In dramatic contrast to the Kodiak giants, brown bears living just a few hundred miles away in the Yukon rarely exceed 330 pounds (150 kg), and those in southern Europe are often under 150 pounds (70 kg). Such huge variation in size might suggest that there is more than one species of brown bear, but in fact the difference probably has more to do with diet than genetics. Bears keep on growing well into adult life, and the rate of growth is highly dependent on the quality of food. Bears that manage to consume a high-protein diet grow much bigger than those forced to survive

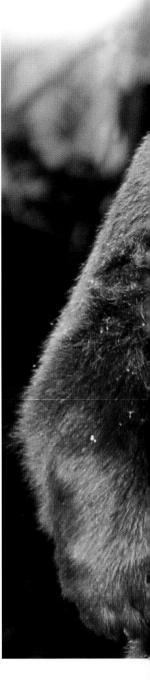

on berries and grass. Kodiak bears and those living on the other side of the Bering Strait in Kamchatka benefit from the annual run of Pacific salmon, which swim upriver in their millions to spawn. For several weeks every summer the bears can gorge themselves on highly nutritious fish, loafing around on the riverbanks between meals and expending little energy. In other parts of the world bears have to survive on much more limited rations, which may also take a good deal of energy to find.

Seasonal Produce

Most brown bears eat more plant material than anything else, carefully selecting the most succulent and nutritious of the season's grasses, fruit, nuts, and fungi. They tend to avoid old-growth vegetation because it is much harder to digest, especially since their gut is basically that of a meat-eater. Brown bears kill and eat other animals—from mice to bison and other bears— as and when the opportunity arises. However, in most parts of their range predatory behavior is rarely planned in advance.

Whether hunting or foraging, the most important bear sense is smell. Compared with its huge black nose, the brown bear's eyes and ears are small, reflecting its relatively poor eyesight and hearing. Large prey animals are usually chased over a short distance at speeds of up to 30 miles per hour (50 km/h), then killed with a mighty blow from the front paws. Large grizzlies are immensely strong and can kill animals as big as horses and cattle, dragging them 100 yards (90 m) or more to feed in a safe place. Attacks on humans are rare, but always well publicized, and will probably become more frequent as the

⊖ *A brown or grizzly bear from the Rocky Mountains. Brown bears vary in size, with the biggest males weighing up to 1,750 pounds (800 kg). Although somewhat lumbering in appearance, even the largest bears can run with surprising speed and agility.*

recreational use of wilderness areas increases. Most attacks involve some kind of provocation; others may be accidental, for example, when a dominant male mistakes a human for a subordinate bear. Mothers with cubs are especially aggressive, but where possible, even they prefer to usher their family away to safety rather than confront a human being. The motivation for an attack appears not to be food, since bears rarely eat their human victims.

Light Sleeper

All brown bears are capable of hibernating, and most do so for between three and seven months of the year. Hibernation is a response to poor weather and lack of food. However, for some southern brown bears conditions never get bad enough to make such a winter retreat worthwhile. Even in northern areas brown bears do not hibernate as deeply as American black bears, and they rouse quickly in response to warmer weather or disturbance of the den. Like American black and polar bears, pregnant female brown bears usually give birth in midwinter. The development of the cubs will only proceed that far if the mother is in a fit condition to rear them. Brown bears reproduce slowly: A female rarely breeds more than once in every three or four years.

Young males disperse up to 60 miles (100 km) from their birthplace. They spend the next few years waiting for the opportunity to replace a resident male or to steal a mating with a receptive female. Young females stay closer to home, often continuing to associate with each other and their mother long after the next batch of cubs is born. Such close family ties make brown bears almost sociable. In parts of the western United States large groups of bears may gather at a food source. Although they interact peacefully most of the time, there is a strict hierarchy, which may be maintained with aggressive displays and fighting.

⊖ *A brown bear fishing for salmon in an Alaskan river. Every summer the bears gorge themselves on the nutritious fish as they swim upriver to spawn.*

The Bear Trade

Bears are popular zoo animals. Some so-called "dancing bears" used to be taken from one town to another to give public performances. However, the decline of brown and black bears was due almost entirely to hunting. In North America the bears were hunted for their fur and to protect livestock. Today hunting is strictly regulated, and bears are treated as game animals rather than a commercial resource. Trading in bear body parts is also restricted by treaty. The threat to bear populations varies from place to place, which is why some animals are officially registered as needing urgent protection, while others are considered to be less at risk.

The most serious threat to bears comes from the Asian medicine trade. Paws, bones, and internal organs are all highly valued, especially the gallbladder, which can fetch over $1,000. Because bear bile is one of the few Asian medicines that may have at least some basis in science, some countries permit the farming of Asiatic black and brown bears. Farmed animals have plastic tubes surgically implanted into their gallbladders so that the bile can be drained off and used without killing the bear. This highly controversial activity is argued by some to reduce the pressure on wild populations, but it also helps perpetuate the use of bear products in the treatment of conditions for which there are a number of effective man-made drugs.

Giant Panda

Ailuropoda melanoleuca

One of the world's most easily recognizable animals, the panda has rarely been seen alive outside China and is now in serious decline. Its distinctive appearance has become the symbol for all animals threatened with extinction.

Common name Giant panda (panda, panda bear)

Scientific name *Ailuropoda melanoleuca*

Family Ursidae

Order Carnivora

Size Length head/body: 47–59 in (120–150 cm); tail length: 5 in (13 cm); height at shoulder: up to 27.5–31 in (70–80 cm)

Weight 165–350 lb (75–160 kg)

Key features Unmistakable large, furry bear with black legs, shoulder band, eye patches, and ears; rest of body is off-white

Habits Solitary; nonterritorial; active between dusk and dawn; climbs well

Breeding One or 2 cubs born August–September after gestation period of 97–163 days (includes variable period of delayed implantation). Weaned at 8–9 months; sexually mature at 6–7 years. May live up to 34 years in captivity, fewer in the wild

Voice Varied sounds, including growls, moans, barks, squeaks, and bleats

Diet Omnivorous, but mostly bamboo and some other plant material; occasionally small animals

Habitat Mountainside forests with bamboo thickets at altitudes of 3,300–13,000 ft (1,000–3,900 m)

Distribution Small remaining range in central China

Status Population: about 1,000; IUCN Endangered; CITES I. Has declined greatly in range and population due to hunting, habitat loss, and specialized lifestyle

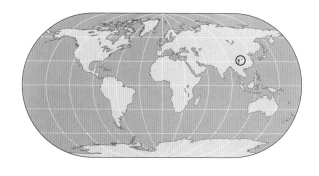

DESPITE BEING NATURALLY RARE and elusive, the giant panda is one of the world's most widely known and best-loved animals. Chinese writings from as long as 3,000 years ago refer to the panda, but the species was unknown to the outside world until 1869, when a skin was sent to the Museum of Natural History in Paris by a French missionary. The species was then formally described, but it was a long time before western scientists were able to see a live one. Even today fewer than 100 pandas have been seen alive in zoos outside China. The name panda is Nepalese, while its former species name, *Ursus melanoleuca*, meant simply "black-and-white bear." *Ailuropoda*, its more recent scientific name, refers to the claws and feet.

Vegetarian Diet

Pandas are almost exclusively vegetarian. However, they evolved from carnivorous ancestors and still have the digestive system of a meat-eater. It includes a short intestine, which is not the best arrangement for digesting the plant material on which pandas mainly feed. Much of the goodness in the panda's diet is never absorbed because meals simply do not spend enough time in the short gut to be properly digested. In order to obtain enough nourishment to survive, the panda has to spend 10 to 12 of its 15 waking hours feeding and eat between 22 and 40 pounds (10 and 18 kg) of bamboo every day. During the bamboo's new

 SEE ALSO Raccoon, Common **1**:22; Panda, Red **1**:30; Old World Monkey Family, The **4**:40

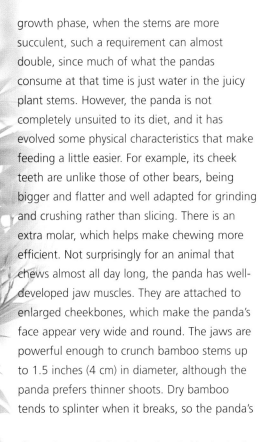

growth phase, when the stems are more succulent, such a requirement can almost double, since much of what the pandas consume at that time is just water in the juicy plant stems. However, the panda is not completely unsuited to its diet, and it has evolved some physical characteristics that make feeding a little easier. For example, its cheek teeth are unlike those of other bears, being bigger and flatter and well adapted for grinding and crushing rather than slicing. There is an extra molar, which helps make chewing more efficient. Not surprisingly for an animal that chews almost all day long, the panda has well-developed jaw muscles. They are attached to enlarged cheekbones, which make the panda's face appear very wide and round. The jaws are powerful enough to crunch bamboo stems up to 1.5 inches (4 cm) in diameter, although the panda prefers thinner shoots. Dry bamboo tends to splinter when it breaks, so the panda's

⊖ *Pandas once inhabited the subtropical lowlands of China, but now can be found only in high-altitude areas where farming and logging have not yet encroached.*

A Bear or Not a Bear?

The panda's relationship to other bears is one of the longest-running puzzles in animal classification. At first sight the animal certainly looks like a bear, and 19th-century zoologists had no hesitation in classifying it in the bear family, Ursidae. However, there is another species of panda, the red or lesser panda (*Ailurus fulgens*), which looks rather like a raccoon. Certain aspects of giant panda physiology are also raccoonlike, and for a while both pandas were placed in the raccoon family, Procyonidae.

Other experts placed them in a family by themselves, the Ailuridae. Modern science has clarified the situation a little. It has revealed that the giant panda's DNA (genetic molecular structure) is more like that of a bear than a raccoon. As a result, the merry-go-round has turned full circle, with most zoologists now agreeing that the giant panda is a rather special kind of bear, or at least an offshoot of the bear family.

Thumbs Up!

The panda's most extraordinary feeding adaptation has nothing to do with its jaws, teeth, or gut. One of the reasons people find the panda so appealing is the way it sits up to eat, clasping a bamboo stem in its paws, much as a human would, rather than browsing off the ground or the growing plant as other herbivores (plant-eating animals) do or lying down and using its mouth to pull its meal to pieces like most carnivores. Bears and their relatives have five digits on each foot, but the thumbs do not oppose the other digits, so they cannot be used to grasp objects the way humans and apes do. The only way most carnivores can hold objects is to clamp them awkwardly between two paws. In order to clasp bamboo shoots the way it does, the panda has developed a new "thumb." It is actually an extension of a bone from its wrist (the radial sesamoid), which grows into a lobe off the main pad on each forefoot. This new thumb is not mobile like a true thumb, but it provides a support against which the panda can press its first two fingers and thereby grip the bamboo stems.

mouth, esophagus, and stomach have an extra thick, leathery lining to prevent injury.

Pandas live alone, but their home ranges often overlap a good deal. They leave scent marks and other signs to indicate their presence, but they take pains not to meet. It may be that the panda's striking black-and-white markings actually help them spot each other at a distance and so avoid getting too close. Keeping spaced out helps ensure they do not compete for the same food supplies. The average panda uses a home range of between 1.5 and 2 square miles (4–6 sq. km) a year, but it rarely moves more than 650 yards (600 m) in the course of a day. Larger movements tend to be seasonal (descending to lower altitudes in winter) or enforced by the cycles of bamboo die-off and regrowth. A stand of bamboo might grow for as long as 100 years before it suddenly flowers, sets seed, and dies back completely. When that happens, the pandas have to move on, or they

⬆ *The panda's extra "thumb" helps it grasp bamboo more easily when feeding. Its habit of picking up food in its paws endears the animal to people.*

⊖ *Giant pandas feed almost entirely on bamboo. When plants die back, the animals must find new sources, but that is becoming increasingly difficult.*

will starve. They are unable to hibernate as some other bears do in times of food shortage because their poor diet does not allow them to build up the necessary fat reserves to sustain them over long periods of inactivity.

Disappearing Habitats

The unpredictable growth cycles of bamboo are not a problem for pandas as long as they are able to move to a new area where there is younger bamboo. But the development of human settlement and agriculture makes doing so very difficult. In the 1970s hundreds of pandas are thought to have starved to death when their bamboos died off, and encroaching farmland meant they had nowhere else to go.

Another serious problem the panda faced in the past was hunting. Panda skins were highly prized for their unusual markings, and various body parts were said to have special medicinal properties. By the late 20th century there were fewer than 1,000 wild pandas left alive. Today the remaining populations are restricted to three small areas in the central Chinese provinces of Shaanxi, Sichuan, and Gansu. They are protected by some of the strictest conservation laws in the world: In the late 1980s the Chinese government sentenced 16 people to life imprisonment and three to death for hunting pandas. There are currently just over 100 pandas living in captivity, the majority in China. Captive-breeding success is low, partly because pandas naturally reproduce very slowly (usually just one cub is successfully reared at a time). Pandas also seem prone to psychological problems in zoos and are reluctant to breed at all. It does not help matters that outside China few countries have more than two pandas. Pandas are such popular attractions that zoos are often unwilling to loan out their animals for breeding purposes. Captive-breeding experts are now turning to technology to help. In the future artificial insemination may be the best way to breed healthy pandas in zoos.

The Hyena Family

Hyenas are dog-sized animals that are found throughout most of Africa. One species (the striped hyena) extends into Arabia and eastward to India. Typical hyenas get most of their food by scavenging and feed mainly on the kills of lions and other large carnivores. The animals have a reputation for being nasty. In fact, they are highly intelligent creatures, often with complex social behavior, and they play a vital role in clearing up the carcasses left by large predators.

What Is a Hyena?

Hyenas are doglike in appearance. They have weak hindquarters and back legs that are shorter than their forelegs. The shoulders are consequently higher than their hips, and the head is carried low, giving the animals a distinctive hunchbacked appearance. The legs are long, and there is a large hairy tail. Typically, the coat color is sandy brown with dark stripes or spots. The jaws are powerful, and typical hyenas have massive crushing and shearing molar teeth for crunching up bones and tough bits of skin. Their digestive juices are so acidic they can digest bone fragments better than any other mammal. By contrast, the aardwolf hyena feeds on insects and has just 24 teeth (typical hyenas have 34). These teeth are small and reduced to simple, widely spaced pointed pegs.

Origins

Since few fossils are known to scientists, the origins of the hyena family are somewhat obscure. Hyenas may have evolved from a relative of the civets (family Viverridae) or an ancient type of mongoose (family Herpestidae). Alternatively, they may have had a separate evolutionary development, quite independent of the other families of carnivores.

Family Hyaenidae: 3 genera, 4 species

Crocuta	1 species, spotted hyena (*C. crocuta*)
Hyaena	2 species, brown hyena (*H. brunnea*); striped hyena (*H. hyaena*)
Proteles	1 species, aardwolf (*P. cristata*)

SEE ALSO Civet and Genet Family, The **1**:88; Mongoose Family, The **1**:98; Zebra, Plains **5**:46

⊕ *A pack of spotted hyenas gather around an elephant carcass. The animals gorge rapidly, consuming 25 to 30 pounds (11 to 14 kg) of flesh at a sitting. Group feeding is noisy, but rarely involves serious fighting.*

Hyenas are mainly nocturnal animals and prefer to rest during the day. However, some species—the spotted hyena for instance—may also be active in the daytime. The animals often shelter in dens among rocks and dense vegetation, sometimes using the abandoned burrows of warthogs or aardvarks.

Cooperative Hunting

Most hyenas live in clans of closely related individuals. Brown and striped hyenas tend to hunt alone, but spotted hyenas often cooperate to kill larger prey than they might otherwise manage. In some places about 90 percent of the spotted hyena's food consists of animals that it kills itself; elsewhere it is only half.

Spotted hyenas can chase their prey for over 2 miles (3 km), reaching speeds of more than 35 miles per hour (60 km/h). They can bring down animals as large as zebras, and soon a noisy pack gathers to grab at the victim, tearing off chunks and swallowing as fast as possible before going off to digest their hasty meals.

Cubs are born in a secure den, which is their operational base for up to 18 months. Spotted hyena cubs (usually twins) are born into a communal den shared with other pups of varying ages. Often there is squabbling among them,

and some pups may be killed as a result of aggressive interactions. Spotted hyenas are born with their teeth well developed. However, they are not fed on meat until they are nearly nine months old. Brown hyenas take meat to their cubs at a much earlier age, sometimes dragging large carcasses back to the den.

To some, the hyena's cringing appearance and weird calls are a sign of evil. Hyenas are often blamed for killing livestock and in the past were killed on sight. Today people are more tolerant, and no hyena species is seriously threatened. Hyenas are particularly common in national parks.

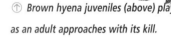

↑ *Brown hyena juveniles (above) play as an adult approaches with its kill.*

← *The aardwolf (left) differs from other hyenas: It feeds on insects, lives in pairs rather than clans, and defends its territory against others of its species.*

Common name Striped hyena

Scientific name *Hyaena hyaena*

Family Hyaenidae

Order Carnivora

Size Length head/body: 39–47 in (100–120 cm); tail length: 10–14 in (25–35 cm); height at shoulder: 26–30 in (66–75 cm)

Weight 55–119 lb (25–54 kg)

Key features A tall, slender hyena with thick neck, large eyes, and bold stripes; fur is long and shaggy with a high hairy crest extending down the middle of the neck and back; face and throat often black; tail white

Habits Solitary or lives in small clans of closely related individuals

Breeding One to 5 (usually 3) cubs born at any time of year after gestation period of 90 days. Weaned at 10 to 12 months; sexually mature at 2–3 years. May live up to 24 years in captivity, probably up to about 15 in the wild

Voice Generally quiet; occasionally growls or whines

Diet An omnivorous scavenger; takes small prey, but may kill larger animals; fruit and bones

Habitat Dry grassland and semidesert; also rocky hills

Distribution North and northeastern Africa; Middle East and Turkey east to India; up to 10,000 ft (3,000 m) in some mountainous areas

Status Population: relatively abundant. Has declined in numbers and distribution, but is still widespread and fairly numerous

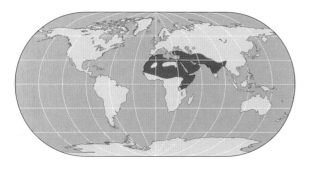

Striped Hyena *Hyaena hyaena*

Smaller in build than its close relative the spotted hyena, the striped hyena's behavior seems to be influenced by its larger, more gregarious cousin.

THE BEHAVIOR OF THE STRIPED HYENA tends to vary according to whether or not spotted hyenas are also present. Where the two species occur together, as they do in parts of northeastern Africa, the striped hyena tends to behave in a quiet and retiring manner and keeps a low profile. Elsewhere the species may be more prominent, sometimes living in large groups. In the northern parts of their geographical range striped hyenas may even hunt in small packs, just as the spotted hyena does farther south.

Clan Boundaries

Like other typical hyenas, the striped hyena sometimes lives in social groups called clans, which are made up of a number of closely related individuals. Each clan has a territory that is carefully marked out with scent produced from an anal pouch under the base of the tail. To deposit a scent marker (a process known as pasting), a hyena stands astride some stiff grass stems and wipes a patch of creamy-white paste onto the vegetation from the lips of its pouch. The process may also be used to mark rocks, shrubs, or pieces of dead wood. The clan will mark its territorial boundary with many thousands of pastings so that any intruding animals from a rival clan will know that they are trespassing. But the scent mark soon loses its smell and needs to be renewed, so members of the clan spend a lot of time patrolling their territory and pasting the grasses and shrubs.

Striped hyenas are sociable animals. When they meet, they erect the crest of long hair that runs down their back and sniff busily at each other. They make a particularly thorough inspection of the anal pouch, which may be turned inside out to assist the process. Close checking of each other's scent credentials not

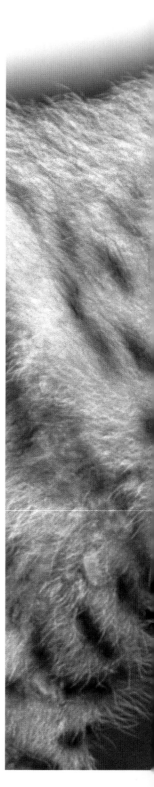

only helps hyenas ensure they belong to the same clan, but probably allows them to recognize each other as individuals. The smell will also convey information about sex, status, and breeding condition. Sometimes the greeting ceremony becomes rather lengthy and violent, especially between strangers. Initially it may involve gentle bites and mock fighting. But subordinate hyenas may be bitten quite hard, held by the throat, and shaken about. An angry hyena will arch its back and raise its hairs on end, often with its tail lifted, making it look much larger than normal.

Striped hyenas live in desert and rocky areas, a generally harsher environment than that enjoyed by the spotted hyena. Such habitat

Striped hyenas are mainly scavengers and, unlike the spotted hyena, tend to forage alone. Since food can often be scarce in their desertlike habitat, the animals try to avoid competing with each other for food sources.

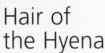

Hair of the Hyena

The hairs on a striped hyena's mane and down the middle of its back are about 8 inches (20 cm) long, three times the length of the hairs on the rest of its body. An angry or excited hyena can make all its hair stand on end and bush out its tail. Standing high on its legs with its back arched, the animal may appear nearly 40 percent larger than usual. Often such an appearance is an effective form of intimidation and enables dominance to be established over subordinate animals without fighting or wasting extra energy.

extends across northern Africa and includes much of the Sahara Desert south to Tanzania, the Middle East as far north as Turkey, and eastward throughout most of India. Although striped hyenas inhabit dry areas, they tend to avoid true desert and make their homes where water is available for at least part of the year. Nevertheless, they can cope with very hot, dry conditions and avoid the heat of the day by being active mainly in the evening or at night. Midday is usually passed in the shade of overhanging rocks or among cool boulders. Some live in rocky areas, others in mountains up to nearly 10,000 feet (3,000 m), where temperatures may fall abruptly after dark.

Striped hyenas can also survive in very cold areas, provided they are also dry. Such bleak habitats often have little food to offer, so the hyenas are forced to range over extremely large areas. They can be found lying up in caves or shallow burrows, or among boulders. Some dens are used for long periods, especially when young are being raised.

Year-Round Breeding

Striped hyenas are capable of breeding from the age of two or three years and usually give birth to about three or four young, occasionally as many as five. Newborn infants weigh about 1.5 pounds (700 g). Striped hyena cubs are born blind, and their eyes do not open for about a week. Births can occur at any time of the year and follow a pregnancy period lasting 90 days. The young are fed on nutritious milk from their mother for the first month of life, after which they will come to rely increasingly on food brought to the den. Nonbreeding subadult animals from previous litters will often help feed the new members of the clan until they are able to fend for themselves, and it is not uncommon for large quantities of bones to accumulate at the entrance to the den.

The nursery den is usually a small collection of tunnels and chambers dug into the ground, but sometimes the animals will use rock crevices for a home. The cubs make a bleating call when they want attention or more food and also when they become excited, especially during play. The nursery den is home to the cubs for up to a year before they become independent from their mother. It takes a long time for the young hyenas to find their way around and learn how to obtain food. Males leave their clan when they become mature and join another social group. It may take a while for the new male to be accepted by the group and to establish sufficient status to gain mating opportunities. Females normally stay with the clan that they were born into and eventually take on the status of their mother.

Threatening Behavior

As the young hyenas get older, their parents become increasingly intolerant of them. When offspring and parents meet, the greeting display needs to include ever more extended appeasement behavior on the part of the younger animals to avoid being attacked by their parents. Subordinate animals show their submissiveness by lowering the head, rolling their eyes, and sometimes lying down. Similar gestures are seen among domestic dogs confronted by dominant animals.

Aggression by dominant hyenas is accompanied by bristling the mane, extending the neck, and sometimes delivering a few sharp nips. Bites are usually aimed at the side of a hyena's neck where the skin is thick, so this kind of biting rarely results in serious wounds. Often minor fights occur, with the animals kneeling down. Fighting in such a way avoids the danger of getting the slender legs broken by an opponent's powerful jaws. Hyenas also threaten each other with growling noises that may rise to barks and be followed by snapping lunges at the opponent's neck.

Cleaning Up

Striped hyenas feed mainly on dead mammals. Food sources may be cattle, horses, or sheep that have died in the harsh, dry conditions. Alternatively, they may be the remains of prey killed by larger predators such as lions. Unlike spotted hyenas, striped hyenas do not benefit

⊕ *Striped hyena cubs live in dens for about a year—until they are independent from their mother. They survive on food brought to the den, often by nonbreeding older brothers and sisters.*

from hunting in large clans. Even so, individual striped hyenas have been known to kill prey up to the size of an adult donkey. However, large mammals are usually too wary to be approached closely and also too strong to be easily killed. Hares, foxes, and large rodents are more common prey. The hyena's powerful jaws can easily cope with crunching up tortoises, grasshoppers, and occasionally smaller insects, such as termites.

Scavengers

Striped hyenas are more omnivorous than other species of their family and often eat wild and cultivated soft fruit and dates if they come across them. They will also eat birds and lizards. Under cover of darkness they often come to scavenge garbage dumps on the outskirts of human settlements. Surplus food may be stored in patches of dense vegetation. However, most of the time food tends to be scarce in the striped hyena's semidesert habitat, so the animals often forage alone to avoid competing with each other. They frequently range over areas of more than 20 square miles (50 sq. km), traveling 19 miles (30 km) in one

⬆ *Striped hyenas check each other's scent credentials in elaborate greeting ceremonies. A meeting between strangers can involve bites and mock fighting or a throat hold in which a subordinate animal is roughly shaken.*

night. Their long legs enable striped hyenas to trot tirelessly at 5 miles per hour (8 km/h) for several hours, sometimes all night.

There are reports of striped hyenas attacking and even killing people—especially children. Yet it is also reported that striped hyenas can become tame and affectionate pets. In some countries parts of the hyena's body are believed to have medicinal value, but in general, human attitudes toward hyenas tend to be rather negative. In North Africa and Arabia, for example, the striped hyena is regarded as a disgusting animal and widely suspected of being a grave robber. It is also unpopular in Israel because of the damage it does to crops of melons, grapes, cucumbers, and other succulent plants that provide moisture as well as food during dry weather. The animals are shot, poisoned, and trapped, but nevertheless manage to remain widespread and fairly abundant.

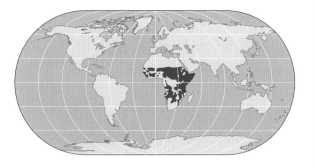

Common name Spotted hyena

Scientific name *Crocuta crocuta*

Family   Hyaenidae

Order   Carnivora

Size   Length head/body: 39–71 in (100–180 cm); tail length: 10–14 in (25–36 cm); height at shoulder: 28–35 in (70–90 cm)

Weight 88–200 lb (40–91 kg); female generally about 12% heavier than male

Key features Doglike, powerfully built animal with short tail and sloping back; pale sandy gray coat with dark, irregular blotches

Habits   Usually nocturnal, but will venture out during the daytime; lives in clans

Breeding   Usually 2, but up to 4 cubs born after gestation period of 4 months. Weaned at 8–18 months; sexually mature at 2 years. May live to over 40 years in captivity, probably fewer in the wild

Voice   Loud whooping noises; crazy-sounding giggle

Diet   Meat from carcasses killed by other predators; slow animals like waterbuck; also tortoises, fish, insects, and garbage

Habitat   Acacia savannas; urban fringes

Distribution Africa south of Sahara, except for areas of thick forest; absent from most of South Africa

Status   Population: several thousand; IUCN Lower Risk: conservation dependent. Widespread and fairly common, but disappearing from many places being unpopular with farmers

Spotted Hyena *Crocuta crocuta*

The spotted hyena has few friends. It is rapidly disappearing from large parts of Africa as a result of its reputation as a killer and undesirable neighbor.

SPOTTED HYENAS LIVE IN SOCIAL groups called clans, which defend a shared territory against rival groups. The clan territory—which may be very large—is staked out with scent marks on logs and boulders. Clans may divide into smaller subgroups and live in a series of burrows that they dig for themselves. Bigger groups occupy a large communal den, often among rocks. Some dens have been used by generations of hyenas over hundreds of years. Although a clan may number over 40 animals, its members seem able to recognize each other, mainly by smell.

Big-Game Hunt

Hyenas are active mainly in the evening and early part of the night. A clan may gang together to kill large mammals such as a wildebeest or zebra. During a chase hyenas are known to manage speeds of 35 miles per hour (60 km/h) or more, but they soon tire and usually give up after less than a mile or so. Only about one-third of such hunts are successful.

Large victims are torn apart, with each hyena greedily swallowing as much as possible in a short time, often as much as 30 pounds (14 kg) of meat. Hyenas will take advantage of sick and injured animals and also pick at carcasses left by lions and other predators. Occasionally, larger groups of hyenas manage to force lions to abandon their fresh kills. Spotted hyenas are also known to exploit the large numbers of young wild antelope and zebra available during the calving season. They may even follow wildebeest herds to pester the females while they are giving birth.

However, most spotted hyenas live in small groups and prefer to forage alone. They may cover up to 50 miles (80 km) in a night, searching for whatever can be picked up with

the least effort. Nowadays that often means garbage scavenged from around the edges of towns and villages, but hyenas will also eat reptiles, eggs, and even large beetles.

Breeding can occur at any time of the year, although only some females have offspring. In a communal den one female is dominant, but others in the same den may be allowed to breed. Young spotted hyenas are born blind and helpless, but develop fast. Only their mother feeds them, providing milk for up to 18 months. She does not normally carry food back to the den, and unlike some hyenas, other females in the clan do not assist in rearing the family. The dominant female is an overbearing individual, and others in the clan will allow her

⊕ *Spotted hyenas are especially good at crunching up fresh bones using their massive jaws and teeth. The shearing teeth are extremely effective and can slice up tough sinews and thick mammal skin better than most knives.*

to eat as much as she wants unchallenged. The general behavior of clan members centers around appeasing the dominant female. She will signal her aggressive mood by raising her tail and sometimes snarling. Unlike all other mammals, her sexual organs look almost exactly like those of a male.

Young hyenas are independent at about 12 to 16 months, and they are sexually mature at two years old. The females generally stay with the clan into which they were born, while the males disperse and join another clan, remaining there for a few years before moving on again. This ensures that the clans do not become inbred. There is no permanent bond between males and females.

Refuse Collectors

Formerly a successful and widespread species, the spotted hyena is still one of the most abundant large African carnivores. However, it has an uneasy relationship with people. Many believe that its weird laughing giggles and manic whoops are associated with evil spirits. Its cringing behavior and habit of scavenging around latrines and garbage dumps make the animal seem unclean. It is also known to attack and eat domestic stock. The spotted hyena has been shot and poisoned wherever land is taken for farming and has become quite rare over large parts of its former range. It is now only really abundant in protected areas such as national parks. Yet it has an important role to play, cleaning up after other animals. By scavenging, ripping apart carcasses, and crunching up bones, the hyena actually helps speed up decomposition.

Common name Aardwolf

Scientific name *Proteles cristata*

Family Hyaenidae

Order Carnivora

Size Length head/body: 22–31 in (55–80 cm); tail length: 8–12 in (20–30 cm); height at shoulder: 16–20 in (40–50 cm)

Weight 18–26 lb (8–12 kg)

Key features Slender, creamy-brown animal with a few widely spaced black stripes; black feet, muzzle, and tail tip; coat often discolored by soil from den; molar teeth small and peglike

Habits Nocturnal; territorial; normally forages alone

Breeding Two to 5 young born after gestation period of about 2–3 months. Weaned at 2–3 months; sexually mature at 1 year. May live up to 20 years in captivity, fewer in the wild

Voice Generally silent, but growls and barks when angry

Diet Mainly termites; some other insects, including beetles and grasshoppers; occasionally mice

Habitat Areas of dry, grazed grassland where termites are abundant

Distribution Southern Africa; separate subspecies in East Africa north to Eritrea

Status Population: widespread, but generally scarce, although not seriously threatened

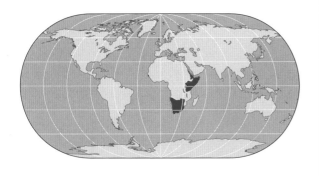

Aardwolf

Proteles cristata

The odd one out among hyenas, the aardwolf feeds on insects, has weak jaws and teeth, and normally lives in pairs or alone.

THE AARDWOLF IS A SPECIALIZED feeder, concentrating on termites. It seems to have evolved from an ancestral form of hyena, becoming different from the typical types about 20 million years ago. Unlike other termite-eating mammals, the aardwolf does not have powerful forelimbs or big claws with which to rip open or dig up termite nests. Instead, it takes harvester termites that normally forage on the surface rather than underground.

Termite Diet

The main food of the aardwolf is two types of termite, which tend to be active at different times of day. The preferred food is the snouted harvester termite, which cannot tolerate exposure to the sun and is therefore active only after dark. In winter or during the wet season they may be hard to find, so the aardwolf switches to another type of harvester termite that tends to be more active during the day.

The availability of harvester termites is the main factor that governs where aardwolves live, and the relative proportions of the nocturnal and diurnal termites (those active by night and day respectively) dictate the activity patterns of the aardwolves themselves.

Harvester termites swarm among dead grass, and aardwolves find them by constantly crisscrossing the ground and listening for the rustling of dry grass stems being invaded by the insect hordes and nibbled by thousands of jaws. The termites are lapped up with masses of sticky saliva. Since termites are only small insects, they do not need to be chewed much, and aardwolves have small, simple teeth (fewer than any other member of the hyena family). An aardwolf may consume nearly a quarter of a million termites in a single night.

⊕ *The termite-eating aardwolf poses no threat to humans or livestock but has been persecuted along with other species of hyena. Yet despite such activities, aardwolf populations remain relatively stable.*

Boundary Marking

Where termites are abundant, aardwolves can manage with smallish territories, sometimes less than 1 square mile (1 to 2 sq. km). Where food is scarce, on the other hand, territories are considerably larger. One territory may include over 3,000 termite nests containing more than 150 million termites. Since the nests are vital to the aardwolves, the animals guard their territories jealously. They mark the boundaries every 50 yards (40–50 m) or so, smearing grass stems with a smelly paste from glands under the tail. They chase off other aardwolves and also jackals, raising the stiff hairs along their back to make themselves look fiercer.

Aardwolves live alone or in pairs and may have up to 10 dens within their home territory. They breed seasonally, giving birth to between two and five cubs. Newborn cubs are helpless, but soon have their eyes open. They stay in the underground den for up to two months, guarded by their father, while the female forages. By the age of three months the cubs are feeding outside the den with one of their parents. They begin to disperse when they can fend for themselves. Before the parents' next family is ready to appear above ground, the cubs move off to find a feeding area of their own.

Aardwolves are harmless and pose no danger to people or livestock. Nevertheless, they have been persecuted along with other hyenas and also killed for their skins (used in tribal ceremonial rugs). In some areas they are at risk from insecticides used to kill locusts; and where termites are eradicated to allow farming, aardwolves cannot survive. Despite such problems, the aardwolf population remains relatively secure.

List of Species

The following lists all species of large carnivores, including their distribution:

Order Carnivora (Part)

FAMILY FELIDAE
Cat Family

Acinonyx

A. jubatus Cheetah; Africa, Middle East

Felis

F. (Profelis) aurata African golden cat; Senegal to Democratic Republic of Congo and Kenya

F. (Catopuma) badia Bay cat (Bornean red cat); Borneo

F. (Prionailurus) bengalensis Leopard cat (Bengal cat); Sumatra, Java, Borneo, Japan, Philippines, Taiwan

F. bieti Chinese desert cat; C. Asia, W. China, S. Mongolia

F. (Lynx) canadensis Canadian lynx; Alaska, Canada, N. U.S.

F. (Caracal) caracal Caracal (lynx, African lynx); Africa and Asia from Turkestan and N.W. India to Arabia

F. chaus Jungle cat; Egypt to Indochina and Sri Lanka

F. (Oncifelis) colocolo Pampas cat; Ecuador to Patagonia

F. (Puma) concolor Puma (cougar, mountain lion, panther); S. Canada to Patagonia

F. (Oncifelis) geoffroyi Geoffroy's cat (Geoffroy's ocelot); Bolivia to Patagonia

F. (Oncifelis) guigna Kodkod (Chilean cat, huiña); C. and S. Chile, W. Argentina

F. (Prionailurus) iriomotensis Iriomote cat; Iriomote and Ryukyu Islands

F. (Oreailurus) jabobita Mountain cat (Andean cat); S. Peru to N. Chile

F. (Lynx) lynx Lynx (Eurasian or northern lynx); W. Europe to Siberia

F. (Otocolobus) manul Pallas's cat (manul); Iran to W. China

F. margarita Sand cat; N. Africa and S.W. Asia (Sahara to Baluchistan)

F. (Pardofelis) marmorata Marbled cat; Sumatra, Borneo; Malaya to Nepal

F. nigripes Black-footed cat; S. Africa, Botswana, Namibia

F. (Leopardus) pardalis Ocelot; Arizona to N. Argentina

F. (Lynx) pardinus Iberian lynx; Spain and Portugal

F. (Prionailurus) planiceps Flat-headed cat; Borneo, Sumatra, Malaya

F. (Prionailurus) rubiginosus Rusty-spotted cat; S. India and Sri Lanka

F. (Lynx) rufus Bobcat (red lynx); S. Canada to S. Mexico

F. (Leptailurus) serval Serval; Africa

F. silvestris Wildcat; W. Europe to India; Africa (*F. s. catus* worldwide, introduced by man)

F. (Catopuma) temmincki Asiatic golden cat (Temminck's golden cat); Nepal to S. China and Sumatra

F. (Leopardus) tigrinus Tiger cat (little spotted cat, ocelot cat, oricilla); Costa Rica to N. Argentina

F. (Prionailurus) viverrinus Fishing cat; Sumatra, Java, to S. China and India

F. (Leopardus) wiedii Margay cat (tigrillo); N. Mexico to N. Argentina

F. (Herpailurus) yaguarondo Jaguarundi (jaguarondi, eyra, otter-cat); Arizona to N. Argentina

Neofelis

N. nebulosa Clouded leopard; India, S. China, Nepal, Myanmar, Indochina to Sumatra and Borneo, possibly also Taiwan (where it may be extinct)

Panthera

P. leo Lion; S. Sahara to S. Africa, excluding Congo rainforest belt; Gujarat, India (a remnant population in Gir Forest Sanctuary)

P. onca Jaguar; S.W. U.S. to C. Patagonia

P. pardus Leopard; Africa south of the Sahara, and S. Asia; scattered populations in N. Africa, Arabia, Far East

P. tigris Tiger; India, S.E. Asia; China; S.E. Russia

P. (Uncia) uncia Snow leopard; C. Asia from the Himalayas to S. and W. Mongolia and S. Russia. Occurs in 12 countries, with China constituting 60 percent of its total range

FAMILY CANIDAE
Dog Family

Canis

C. adustus Side-striped jackal; throughout C. Africa extending into parts of E. and W. Africa

C. aureus Golden jackal (common jackal); from N. and E. Africa through to the Middle East, S.E. Europe, and on into Asia

C. dingo Dingo; Australasia, including Indonesia (part); Malaysia, Thailand, and Myanmar

C. latrans Coyote (prairie or brush wolf); America from N. Alaska to Costa Rica

C. lupus Gray wolf (timber or white wolf); N. America; Europe; Asia; Middle East

C. mesomelas Black-backed jackal (silver-backed jackal); two separate populations, one in E. Africa, one in S. Africa. Does not occur in C. Africa

C. rufus Red wolf; S.E. U.S.

C. simensis Ethiopian wolf (Simien fox or Simien jackal); mountains of central Ethiopia

Chrysocyon

C. brachyurus Maned wolf; C. and S. Brazil, Paraguay, N. Argentina, E. Bolivia, S.E. Peru

Cuon

C. alpinus Dhole (Asian wild dog or red dog); W. Asia to China, India, Indochina to Java. Rare outside protected areas

Dusicyon South American foxes (zorros)

D. (Pseudalopex) culpaeus Colpeo zorro; Andes from Ecuador and Peru to Tierra del Fuego

D. (Pseudalopex) fulvipes Darwin's zorro; Chiloe Island and Nahuel Huapi National Park, Chile

D. (Pseudalopex) griseus Argentine gray zorro (gray or pampas fox); distribution as colpeo, but at lower altitudes in Ecuador and N. Chile

D. (Pseudalopex) gymnocercus Azara's zorro (pampas fox); Paraguay, Chile, S.E. Brazil south through E. Argentina to Rio Negro

D. (Atelocynus) microtis Small-eared zorro (small-eared dog, zorro negro); Amazon and Orinoco Basins, parts of Peru, Colombia, Ecuador, Venezuela, Brazil

D. (Pseudalopex) sechurae Sechuran zorro; N. Peru and S. Ecuador

D. (Cerdocyon) thous Crab-eating zorro (crab-eating fox or common zorro); Colombia and Venezuela to N. Argentina and Paraguay

D. (Pseddalopex) vetulus Hoary fox (small-toothed dog); S.C. Brazil

Lycaon

L. pictus African wild dog (wild dog, painted dog, or African hunting dog); Africa from the Sahara to S. Africa

Nyctereutes

N. procyonoides Raccoon dog; E. Asia, in Far East, E. Siberia, Manchuria, China, Korea, Japan, and N. Indochinese Peninsula; introduced to Europe

Otocyon

O. megalotis Bat-eared fox (Delandi's fox); two populations, one from S. Zambia to S. Africa, the other from Ethiopia to Tanzania

Speothos

S. venaticus Bush dog (vinegar fox); Panama to Guyana and through Brazil

Urocyon Gray foxes

U. cinereoargenteus Gray fox (tree fox); C. U.S. to the prairies south to Venezuela north to Ontario

U. littoralis Island gray fox; islands of W. U.S.

Vulpes Vulpine foxes

V. bengalensis Indian fox (Bengal fox); India, Pakistan, and Nepal

V. cana Blanford's fox (hoary or Afghan fox); Afghanistan, S.W. Russian Federation, Turkmenistan, N.E. Iran, Baluchistan; isolated population in Israel

V. chama Cape fox (silverbacked fox); Africa south of Zimbabwe and Angola

V. corsac Corsac fox; S.E. Russian Federation, Turkestan, Mongolia, Transbaikalia to N. Manchuria and N. Afghanistan

V. ferrilata Tibetan fox (Tibetan sand fox); Tibet and Nepal

V. (Alopex) lagopus Arctic fox (polar, blue, or white fox); circumpolar in tundra latitudes

V. macrotis Kit fox; N.W. Mexico and S.W. U.S.

V. pallida Pale fox; N. Africa from Red Sea to Atlantic, Senegal to Sudan and Somalia

V. rüppelli Rüppell's fox (sand fox); scattered populations between Morocco and Afghanistan, N.E. Nigeria, N. Cameroon, Chad, Central African Republic, Gabon, Congo, Somalia, Sudan, Egypt, Sinai, Arabia

V. velox Swift fox (kit fox); C. U.S. from Texas to South Dakota; reintroduced into Canada and Montana

V. vulpes Red fox (silver or cross fox); N. Hemisphere from Arctic Circle to N. African and C. American deserts and Asiatic steppes, (natural southern limit in Sudan); introduced to Australia

V. (Fennecus) zerda Fennec fox; N. Africa throughout Sahara east to Sinai and Arabia

FAMILY URSIDAE

Bear Family

Ailuropoda

A. melanoleuca Giant panda (panda bear, bamboo bear, or panda); Sichuan, Shaanxi, and Gansu provinces of C. and W. China

Helarctos

H. (Ursus) malayanus Sun bear (Malayan sun bear, Malay bear, honey bear, dog bear); S.E. Asia, Sumatra, Borneo; isolated patches in E. India and S. China

Melursus

M. (Ursus) ursinus Sloth bear (honey bear, lip or labiated bear, aswail); India, Nepal, Bhutan, Sri Lanka, and possibly Bangladesh

Tremarctos

T. ornatus Andean bear (spectacled bear, ucumari); Andes from W. Venezuela to Bolivia-Argentina border

Ursus

U. arctos Brown bear (grizzly or kodiak bear); N.W. N. America, Scandinavia through Russia to Japan; scattered in S. and E. Europe, Middle East, Himalayas, China, and Mongolia

U. americanus American black bear; throughout Canada, U.S. except central Plains states, N. Mexico

U. maritimus Polar bear; circumpolar Arctic

U. thibetanus Asian black bear (Asiatic black bear, moon bear, white-breasted bear); Iran to S.E. Asia, Taiwan (formosan black bear), gap in C. China continuing in N. China, E. Siberia, and Japan

FAMILY HYAENIDAE

Hyena Family

Crocuta

C. crocuta Spotted hyena (laughing hyena); Sub-Saharan Africa, except Congo rain forests and far south

Hyaena

H. (Parahyaena) brunnea Brown hyena (beach or strand wolf); widespread in S. Africa, particularly in the west; also into S. Angola

H. hyaena Striped hyena; N.W. and N.E. Africa, Syria, Asia Minor, Caucasus, India, Arabia

Proteles

P. cristata Aardwolf; S. Africa and E. Africa

Glossary

Words in SMALL CAPITALS refer to other entries in the glossary.

Adaptation features of an animal that adjust it to its environment; may be produced by evolution—e.g., camouflage coloration

Adaptive radiation when a group of closely related animals (e.g., members of a FAMILY) have evolved differences from each other so that they can survive in different NICHES

Adult a fully grown animal that has reached breeding age

Anal gland (anal sac) a gland opening by a short duct either just inside the anus or on either side of it

Antler branched prongs on the head of male deer, made of solid bone

Arboreal living among the branches of trees

Arthropod animals with a jointed outer skeleton, e.g., crabs and insects

Biodiversity a variety of SPECIES and the variation within them

Biomass the total weight of living material

Biped any animal that walks on two legs. See QUADRUPED

Breeding season the entire cycle of reproductive activity from courtship, pair formation (and often establishment of TERRITORY), through nesting to independence of young

Browsing feeding on leaves of trees and shrubs

Cache a hidden supply of food; also (verb) to hide food for future use

Callosities hardened, thickened areas on the skin (e.g., ischial callosities in some PRIMATES)

Canine (tooth) a sharp stabbing tooth usually longer than rest

Canopy continuous (closed) or broken (open) layer in forests produced by the intermingling of branches of trees

Capillaries tiny blood vessels that convey blood through organs from arteries to veins

Carnassial (teeth) opposing pair of teeth especially adapted to shear with a cutting (scissorlike) edge; in living mammals the arrangement is unique to Carnivora, and the teeth involved are the fourth upper PREMOLAR and first lower MOLAR

Carnivore meat-eating animal

Carrion dead animal matter used as a food source by scavengers

Cecum a blind sac in the digestive tract opening out from the junction between the small and large intestines. In herbivorous mammals it is often very large; it is the site of bacterial action on CELLULOSE. The end of the cecum is the appendix; in SPECIES with a reduced cecum the appendix may retain an antibacterial function

Cellulose the material that forms the cell walls of plants

Cementum hard material that coats the roots of mammalian teeth. In some SPECIES cementum is laid down in annual layers that, under a microscope, can be counted to estimate the age of individuals

Cheek teeth teeth lying behind the CANINES in mammals, consisting of PREMOLARS and MOLARS

CITES Convention on International Trade in Endangered Species. An agreement between nations that restricts international trade to permitted levels through licensing and administrative controls. Rare animals and plants are assigned to categories: (for example Appendix 1, 2). See Volume 1 page 17

Cloven hoof foot that is formed from two toes, each within a horny covering

Congenital condition animal is born with

Coniferous forest evergreen forests of northern regions and mountainous areas dominated by pines, spruces, and cedars

Corm underground food storage bulb of certain plants

Crepuscular active in twilight

Cursorial adapted for running

Deciduous forest dominated by trees that lose their leaves in winter (or the dry season)

Deforestation the process of cutting down and removing trees for timber or to create open space for activities such as growing crops and grazing animals

Delayed implantation when the development of a fertilized egg is suspended for a variable period before it implants into the wall of the UTERUS and completes normal pregnancy. Births are thus delayed until a favorable time of year

Den a shelter, natural or constructed, used for sleeping, giving birth, and raising young; also (verb) the act of retiring to a DEN to give birth and raise young or for winter shelter

Dental formula a convention for summarizing the dental arrangement, in which the numbers of all types of tooth in each half of the upper and lower jaw are given. The numbers are always presented in the order: INCISOR (I), CANINE (C), PREMOLAR (P), MOLAR (M). The final figure is the total number of teeth to be found in the skull. A typical example for Carnivora is I3/3, C1/1, P4/4, M3/3 = 44

Dentition animal's set of teeth

Desert area of low rainfall dominated by specially adapted plants such as cacti

Diastema a space between the teeth, usually the INCISORS and CHEEK TEETH. It is typical of rodents and lagomorphs, although also found in UNGULATES

Digit a finger or toe

Digitigrade method of walking on the toes without the heel touching the ground. See PLANTIGRADE

Dispersal the scattering of young animals going to live away from where they were born and brought up

Display any relatively conspicuous pattern of behavior

that conveys specific information to others, usually to members of the same SPECIES; can involve visual or vocal elements, as in threat, courtship, or greeting displays

Diurnal active during the day

DNA (deoxyribonucleic acid) the substance that makes up the main part of the chromosomes of all living things; contains the genetic code that is handed down from generation to generation

DNA analysis "genetic fingerprinting," a technique that allows scientists to see who is related to whom, for example, which male was the father of particular offspring

Domestication process of taming and breeding animals to provide help and useful products for humans

Dorsal relating to the back or spinal part of the body; usually the upper surface

Droppings see FECES and SCATS

Ecosystem a whole system in which plants, animals, and their environment interact

Edentate toothless, but is also used as group name for anteaters, sloths, and armadillos

Endemic found only in one small geographical area and nowhere else

Estrus the period when eggs are released from the female's ovaries, and she becomes available for successful mating. Estrous females are often referred to as "in heat" or as "RECEPTIVE" to males

Eutherian mammals that give birth to babies, not eggs, and rear them without using a pouch on the mother's belly

Extinction process of dying out in which every last individual dies, and the SPECIES is lost forever

Eyeshine where the eyes of animals (especially CARNIVORES) reflect a beam of light shone at them. This is caused by a special reflective layer (the tapetum) at the back of the eye characteristic of many NOCTURNAL species and associated with increased abilities to see in dark

Family technical term for a group of closely related SPECIES that often also look quite similar. Zoological family names always end in "idae." See Volume 1 page 11. Also used as the word for a social group within a species consisting of parents and their offspring

Feces remains of digested food expelled from the body as pellets. Often accompanied by SCENT secretions

Feral domestic animals that have gone wild and live independently of people

Flystrike where CARRION-feeding flies have laid their eggs on an animal

Fossorial adapted for digging and living in burrows or underground tunnels

Frugivore an animal that eats fruit as main part of the diet

Fur mass of hairs forming a continuous coat characteristic of mammals

Fused joined together

Gape wide-open mouth

Gene the basic unit of heredity enabling one generation to pass on characteristics to its offspring

Generalist an animal that is capable of a wide range of activities, not specialized

Genus a group of closely related SPECIES. The plural of genus is genera. See Volume 1 page 11

Gestation the period of pregnancy between fertilization of the egg and birth of the baby

Grazing feeding on grass

Gregarious living together in loose groups or herds

Harem a group of females living in the same TERRITORY and consorting with a single male

Herbivore an animal that eats plants (grazers and browsers are thus herbivores)

Heterodont DENTITION specialized into CANINES, INCISORS, and PREMOLARS, each type of tooth having a different function. See HOMODONT

Hibernation becoming inactive in winter, with lowered body temperature to save energy. Hibernation takes place in a special nest or DEN called a hibernaculum

Homeothermy maintenance of a high and constant body temperature by means of internal processes; also called "warm-blooded"

Home range the area that an animal uses in the course of its normal periods of activity. See TERRITORY

Homodont DENTITION in which the teeth are all similar in appearance and function

Horns a pair of sharp, unbranched prongs projecting from the head of CLOVEN-HOOFED animals. Horns have a bony core with a tough outer covering made of KERATIN like our fingernails

Hybrid offspring of two closely related SPECIES that can interbreed, but the hybrid is sterile and cannot produce offspring of its own

Inbreeding breeding among closely related animals (e.g., cousins) leading to weakened genetic composition and reduced survival rates

Incisor (teeth) simple pointed teeth at the front of the jaws used for nipping and snipping

Indigenous living naturally in a region; NATIVE (i.e., not an introduced SPECIES)

Insectivore animals that feed on insects and similar small prey. Also used as a group name for animals such as hedgehogs, shrews, and moles

Interbreeding breeding between animals of different SPECIES or varieties within a single FAMILY or strain; interbreeding can cause dilution of the gene pool

Interspecific between SPECIES

Intraspecific between individuals of the same SPECIES

Invertebrates animals that have no backbone (or other true bones) inside their body, e.g., mollusks, insects, jellyfish, and crabs

IUCN International Union for the Conservation of Nature, responsible for assigning animals and plants to internationally agreed categories of rarity. See table below

Juvenile a young animal that has not yet reached breeding age

Keratin tough, fibrous material that forms hairs, feathers, and protective plates on the skin of VERTEBRATE animals

Lactation process of producing milk in MAMMARY GLANDS for offspring

Larynx voice box where sounds are created

Latrine place where FECES are left regularly, often with SCENT added

Leptospirosis disease caused by leptospiral bacteria in kidneys and transmitted via urine

Mammary glands characteristic of mammals, glands for production of milk

Marine living in the sea

Matriarch senior female member of a social group

Metabolic rate the rate at which chemical activities occur within animals, including the exchange of gasses in respiration and the liberation of energy from food

Metabolism the chemical activities within animals that turn food into energy

Migration movement from one place to another and back again, usually seasonal

Molars large crushing teeth at the back of the mouth

Molt the process in which mammals shed hair, usually seasonal

Monogamous animals that have only one mate at a time

Montane in a mountain environment

Mustelid small CARNIVORE (e.g., weasel) belonging to the FAMILY Mustelidae

Mutation random changes in genetic material

IUCN CATEGORIES

EX **Extinct**, when there is no reasonable doubt that the last individual of a species has died.

EW **Extinct in the Wild**, when a species is known only to survive in captivity or as a naturalized population well outside the past range.

CR **Critically Endangered**, when a species is facing an extremely high risk of extinction in the wild in the immediate future.

EN **Endangered**, when a species faces a very high risk of extinction in the wild in the near future.

VU **Vulnerable**, when a species faces a high risk of extinction in the wild in the medium-term future.

LR **Lower Risk**, when a species has been evaluated and does not satisfy the criteria for CR, EN, or VU.

DD **Data Deficient**, when there is not enough information about a species to assess the risk of extinction.

NE **Not Evaluated**, species that have not been assessed by the IUCN criteria.

Native belonging to that area or country, not introduced by human assistance

Natural selection when animals and plants are challenged by natural processes (including predation and bad weather) to ensure survival of the fittest

New World the Americas; OLD WORLD refers to the non-American continents (not usually Australia)

Niche part of a habitat occupied by an ORGANISM, defined in terms of all aspects of its lifestyle

Nocturnal active at night

Nomadic animals that have no fixed home, but wander continuously

Old World non-American continents. See NEW WORLD

Omnivore an animal that eats almost anything, meat or vegetable

Opportunistic taking advantage of every varied opportunity that arises; flexible behavior

Opposable fingers or toes that can be brought to bear against others on the same hand or foot in order to grip objects

Order a subdivision of a class of animals consisting of a series of related animal FAMILIES. See Volume 1 page 11

Organism any member of the animal or plant kingdom; a body that has life

Ovulation release of egg from the female's ovary prior to its fertilization

Pair bond behavior that keeps a male and a female together beyond the time it takes to mate; marriage is a "pair bond"

Parasite an animal or plant that lives on or within the body of another

Parturition process of giving birth

Pelage furry coat of a mammal

Pelt furry coat; often refers to skin removed from animal as fur

Pheromone SCENT produced by animals to enable others to find and recognize them

Physiology the processes and workings within plants and animal bodies, e.g., digestion. Maintaining a warm-blooded state is a part of mammal physiology

Placenta the structure that links an embryo to its mother during pregnancy, allowing exchange of chemicals between them

Plantigrade walking on the sole with the heels touching the ground. See DIGITIGRADE

Polygamous when animals have more than one mate in a single mating season. MONOGAMOUS animals have only a single mate

Polygynous when a male mates with several females in one BREEDING SEASON

Population a distinct group of animals of the same SPECIES or all the animals of that species

Posterior the hind end or behind another structure

Predator an animal that kills live prey for food

Prehensile grasping tail or fingers

Premolars teeth found in front of the MOLARS, but behind the CANINES

Pride social group of lions

Primate a group of mammals that includes monkeys, apes, and ourselves

Promiscuous mating often with many mates, not just one

Protein chemicals made up of amino acids. Essential in the diet of animals

Quadruped an animal that walks on all fours (a BIPED walks on two legs)

Range the total geographical area over which a SPECIES is distributed

Receptive when a female is ready to mate (in ESTRUS)

Reproduction the process of breeding, creating new offspring for the next generation

Retina light-sensitive layer at the back of the eye

Retractile capable of being withdrawn, as in the claws of typical cats, which can be folded back into the paws to protect them from damage when walking

Riparian living beside rivers and lakes

Roadkill animals killed by road traffic

Rumen complex stomach found in RUMINANTS specifically for digesting plant material

Ruminant animals that eat vegetation and later bring it back from the stomach to chew again ("chewing the cud" or "rumination") to assist its digestion by microbes in the stomach

Savanna tropical grasslands with scattered trees and low rainfall, usually in warm areas

Scats fecal pellets, especially of CARNIVORES. SCENT is often deposited with the pellets as territorial markers

Scent chemicals produced by animals to leave smell messages for others to find and interpret

Scrotum bag of skin within which the male testicles are located

Scrub vegetation dominated by shrubs—woody plants usually with more than one stem

Secondary forest trees that have been planted or grown up on cleared ground

Siblings brothers and sisters

Social behavior interactions between individuals within the same SPECIES, e.g., courtship

Species a group of animals that look similar and can breed to produce fertile offspring

Spraint hunting term for SCATS (see above) of certain CARNIVORES, especially otters

Steppe open grassland in parts of the world where the climate is too harsh for trees to grow

Sub-Saharan all parts of Africa lying south of the Sahara Desert

Subspecies a locally distinct group of animals that differ slightly from the normal appearance of the SPECIES; often called a race

Symbiosis when two or more SPECIES live together for their mutual benefit more successfully than either could live on its own

Taxonomy the branch of biology concerned with classifying ORGANISMS into groups according to similarities in their structure, origins, or behavior. The categories, in order of increasing broadness, are: SPECIES, GENUS, FAMILY, ORDER, class, and phylum. See Volume 1 page 11

Terrestrial living on land

Territory defended space

Thermoregulation the maintenance of a relatively constant body temperature either by adjustments to METABOLISM or by moving between sunshine and shade

Translocation transferring members of a SPECIES from one location to another

Tundra open grassy or shrub-covered lands of the far north

Underfur fine hairs forming a dense, woolly mass close to the skin and underneath the outer coat of stiff hairs in mammals

Ungulate hoofed animals such as pigs, deer, cattle, and horses; mostly HERBIVORES

Uterus womb in which embryos of mammals develop

Ventral the belly or underneath of an animal (opposite of DORSAL)

Vertebrate animal with a backbone (e.g., fish, mammals, reptiles), usually with skeleton made of bones, but sometimes softer cartilage

Vibrissae sensory whiskers, usually on snout, but can be on areas such as elbows, tail, or eyebrows

Viviparous animals that give birth to active young rather than laying eggs

Vocalization making of sounds such as barking and croaking

Zoologist person who studies animals

Zoology the study of animals

Further Reading

General

Cranbrook, G., **The Mammals of Southeast Asia**, Oxford University Press, New York, NY, 1991

Eisenberg, J. F., and Redford, K. H., **The Mammals of the Neotropics**, University of Chicago Press, Chicago, IL, 1999

Estes, R. D., **The Behavioral Guide to African Mammals**, University of California Press, Berkley, CA, 1991

Kingdon, J., **The Kingdon Field Guide to African Mammals**, Academic Press, San Diego, CA, 1997

MacDonald, D., **Collins Field Guide to the Mammals of Britain and Europe**, Harper Collins, New York, NY, 1993

MacDonald, D., **The Encyclopedia of Mammals**, Barnes and Noble, New York, NY, 2001

Nowak, R. M., **Walker's Mammals of the World**, The John Hopkins University Press, Baltimore, MD., 1999

Whitaker, J. O., **National Audubon Society Field Guide to North American Mammals**, Alfred A. Knopf, New York, NY, 1996

Wilson, D. E., **The Smithsonian Book of North American Mammals**, Smithsonian Institution Press, Washington, DC, 1999

Wilson, D. E., and Reeder, D.M., **Mammal Species of the World. A Taxonomic and Geographic Reference**, Smithsonian Institution Press, Washington, DC, 1999

Young, J. Z., **The Life of Mammals: Their Anatomy and Physiology**, Oxford University Press, Oxford, U.K., 1975

Specific to this volume

Alderton, D., **Cats**, Dorling Kindersley, New York, NY, 2000

Alderton, D., **Foxes, Wolves, and Wild Dogs of the World**, Blandford, U.K., 1998

Caro, T., **Cheetahs of the Serengeti Plains**, Chicago University Press, Chicago, IL, 1994

Creel, S., and Creel, N., **The African Wild Dog**, Princeton University Press, Princeton, NJ, 2002

De La Rosa, C., and Nocke, C., **A Guide to the Carnivores of Central America**, University of Texas Press, Austin, TX, 2000

Gittelman, J. L., **Carnivore Behavior, Ecology, and Evolution**, Cornell University Press, Ithaca, NY, 1996

Gittelman, J. L., **Carnivore Conservation**, Cambridge University Press, U.K., 2001

Jones, K., **Wolf Mountains**, Calgary University Press, Calgary, Canada, 2002

Kitchener, A., **The Natural History of Wildcats**, Cornell University Press, Ithaca, NY, 1991

Kruuk, H., **The Spotted Hyena**, University of Chicago Press, Chicago, IL, 1972

MacDonald, D., **The Velvet Claw**, B.B.C. Books, London, U.K., 1992

Mech, L. D., **The Wolf: Ecology and Behavior of an Endangered Species**, Minnesota University Press, Minneapolis, MN, 1981

McIntyre, R., **War Against the Wolf**, Voyageur Press, Stillwater, MN, 1995

Schaller, G. B., **The Serengeti Lion**, Chicago University Press, Chicago, IL, 1976

Schaller, G. B., **The Giant Pandas of Wolong**, University of Chicago Press, Chicago, IL, 1985

Servheen, C., **Bears: Status Survey and Conservation Action Plan**, IUCN, Switzerland and Cambridge, U.K., 1999

Sunquist, M., and Sunquist, F., **Wildcats of the World**, Chicago University Press, Chicago, IL, 2002

Turner, D. C., **The Domestic Cat**, Cambridge University Press, U.K., 2000

Useful Websites

General

http://animaldiversity.ummz.umich.edu/
University of Michigan Museum of Zoology animal diversity websites. Search for pictures and information about animals by class, family, and common name. Includes glossary

http://www.cites.org/
IUCN and CITES listings. Search for animals by scientific name, order, family, genus, species, or common name. Location by country; explanation of reasons for listings

http://endangered.fws.gov
Information about threatened animals and plants from the U.S. Fish and Wildlife Service, the organization in charge of 94 million acres (38 million ha) of American wildlife refuges

http://www.iucn.org
Details of species and their status; listings by the International Union for the Conservation of Nature, also lists IUCN publications

http://www.nccnsw.org.au
Website for threatened Australian species

http://www.ewt.org.za
Website for threatened South African wildlife

http://www.panda.org
World Wide Fund for Nature (WWF), newsroom, press releases, government reports, campaigns

http://www.aza.org
American Zoo and Aquarium Association

http://www.ultimateungulate.com
Guide to world's hoofed mammals

http://www.wcs.org
Website of the Wildlife Conservation Society

http://www.nwf.org
Website of the National Wildlife Federation

http://www.nmnh.si.edu/msw/
www.nmnh.si.edu/msw/
Mammals list on Smithsonian Museum site

Specific to this volume

http://www.carnivoreconservation.org/
News, links, recent books, etc., on carnivore ecology and conservation

http://www.defenders.org/
Active conservation of carnivores, including wolves and grizzly bears

http://www.wwfcanada.org/en/res_links
/pdf/projdesc.pdf
Carnivore conservation in Rocky Mountains

http://www.5tigers.org
Comprehensive information about tigers

http://www.wildlifetrustofindia.org
Information about Indian wildlife, including tigers

http://www.liberalmafia.org/hyenas/
hyena.html
An information website on hyenas, with facts and photos for spotted hyenas, brown hyenas, and aardwolves

Set Index

A **bold** number shows the volume and is followed by the relevant page numbers (e.g., **1**: 52, 74).

Common names in **bold** (e.g., **aardwolf**) mean that the animal has an illustrated main entry in the set. Underlined page numbers (e.g., **9**: 78–79) refer to the main entry for that animal.

Italic page numbers (e.g., **2**: *103*) point to illustrations of animals in parts of the set other than the main entry.

Page numbers in parentheses—e.g., **1**: (24)—locate information in At-a-Glance boxes.

Animals that get main entries in the set are indexed under their common names, alternative common names, and scientific names.

A

aardvark 1: *10*; **5**: (10), (12); **9**: 64, 65, (66), 67, <u>78–79</u>
  African **9**: 65
aardwolf 2: 102, *103*, <u>110–111</u>
Abrocoma bennetti **8**: 30
Abrocomidae **8**: 31
acacia **6**: 87
Acinonyx
  A. jubatus **2**: 10, <u>26–29</u>
  A. rex **2**: 29
Aconaemys fuscus **8**: 30
acouchi **7**: *12*
  red **8**: 30
Acrobates pygmaeus **10**: 74, <u>84–85</u>
Acrobatidae **10**: (76)
addax **6**: 62
Addax nasomaculatus **6**: 62
Aepyceros melampus **6**: 62, <u>86–87</u>
Aepyprymnus rufescens **10**: 48
Aeromys tephromelas **7**: 34, 36
Africa, national parks/reserves **2**: 16, 31; **5**: 34
Afrotheres **5**: (10)
Afrotheria **9**: 10
agouti 7: 8, *10*, *12*, 14; **8**: 28
  black **8**: <u>8–9</u>
  Central American **8**: 30
  common 8: <u>42–43</u>
  spotted (common) **8**: <u>42–43</u>
Agouti
  A. paca **8**: 30
  A. taczanowskii **8**: 30
Agoutidae **7**: *12*
agriculture **1**: 46; **2**: 21, 28, 44, 69, 77, 79
Ailuridae **2**: (99)
Ailurinae **1**: 20
Ailuropoda melanoleuca **2**: 82, <u>98–101</u>
Ailurops ursinus **10**: 74
Ailurus fulgens **1**: 20, <u>30–31</u>; **2**: (99)
alarm calls **4**: 46, 57, 89, 100; **6**: 79; **7**: 53, 111; **8**: 51, 55, 99
  see also communication
albino **8**: (84)
Alcelaphus
  A. buselaphus **6**: 62
  A. lichtensteinii **6**: 62
Alces
  A. alces **6**: 10, <u>14–19</u>
  A. alces alces **6**: 15
  A. alces americanus **6**: 15
  A. alces andersoni **6**: 15
  A. alces gigas **6**: 15
  A. alces shirasi **6**: 15
Allenopithecus nigroviridis **4**: 40
Allocebus trichotis **4**: 96
Alopex lagopus see *Vulpes lagopus*
Alouatta
  A. fusca **4**: 72, <u>74–75</u>

  A. palliata **4**: 72
  A. seniculus **4**: 72
alpaca **5**: 92, 93, 105, (106)
ambergris **3**: 89
Amblonyx cinereus **1**: 32, <u>70–71</u>
American Sign Language **4**: 13, (16), 27
Ammodorcas clarkei **6**: 62
Ammotragus lervia **6**: 62
angwantibo **4**: 106, *106*
animal farming **2**: (97)
anoa, lowland **6**: 62
Anomaluridae **7**: *12*, (19)
anteater 1: 9, 14; **9**: <u>64–67</u>
  banded *see* numbat
  giant 9: *64*, 65, <u>68–71</u>
  marsupial *see* numbat
  short-nosed spiny *see* echidna, short-beaked
  silky **9**: 65, 66
Antechinomys laniger **10**: 27
antechinus 10: 11, 25, 20, (25), 27
  agile **10**: 41
  brown 10: 27, <u>40–41</u>
  dusky **10**: 27
  sandstone **10**: 27
Antechinus
  A. stuartii **10**: 27, <u>40–41</u>
  A. swainsonii **10**: 27
antelope 5: 10, *11*, 12, 13; **6**: <u>60–63</u>
  American pronghorn **2**: 26; **6**: 63
  four-horned **6**: 60, 62
  pronghorn 6: 60, 62, (63), <u>110–111</u>
  pygmy **6**: 60, 62
  roan **6**: 62
  royal **6**: 60, 62
  sable **6**: 62
  Tibetan **6**: 62
Antidorcas marsupialis **6**: 62, <u>96–97</u>
Antilocapra americana **6**: 62, <u>110–111</u>
Antilocapridae **6**: 63, 110
Antilope cervicapra **6**: 62
antlers **6**: 9, 12, (15), 24–25, 34, 38, 40, *60*
ants **9**: 64, 66, 69, 76
Aonyx
  A. capensis **1**: 32
  A. cinereus see *Amblonyx cinereus*
  A. congicus **1**: 32
Aotus
  A. nigriceps **4**: 72
  A. trivirgatus **4**: 72, <u>84–85</u>
ape
  ape family 4: <u>12–13</u>
  Barbary *see* macaque, Barbary
  red *see* orangutan
Aplodontia rufa **7**: 28
Aplodontidae **7**: *12*, 28, 29
Apodemus sylvaticus **7**: <u>78–79</u>
Appaloosa **5**: 59
archaeocetes **3**: 56

Archaeonycteris **1**: *8*
Arctictis binturong **1**: 88
Arctocebus **4**: 106
  A. aureus **4**: 106
  A. calabarensis **4**: 106
Arctocephalus
  A. gazella **3**: 9
  A. pusillus **3**: 9, <u>16–17</u>
Arctogalidia trivirgata **1**: 88
Arctonyx collaris **1**: 32
Argentinosaurus huinculensis **3**: 98
Arjin Shan Lop Nur Nature Reserve **5**: (102)
armadillo 9: <u>64–67</u>
  common **9**: 65
  giant **9**: 65
  lesser fairy **9**: 65
  long-nosed (nine-banded) **9**: 65, <u>74–77</u>
  nine-banded 9: 65, <u>74–77</u>
  southern naked-tailed **9**: 65, 66
  three-banded **9**: 64
artiodactyl **1**: *8*; **8**: 102
Artiodactyla **1**: *10*; **5**: (10), 12, 66; **6**: 52
Arvicola terrestris **7**: <u>98–99</u>
Aspilia **4**: (29)
ass 5: 42, (44)
  African **5**: 42
  Asian wild 5: <u>56–57</u>
  Asiatic **5**: 42
  domestic **5**: 57
Atelerix
  A. albiventris **9**: 12, <u>20–21</u>
  A. algirus **9**: 12, *13*
  A. frontalis **9**: 21
Ateles
  A. belzebuth **4**: 72
  A. geoffroyi **4**: 72, <u>76–77</u>
Atherurus
  A. africanus **8**: 12
  A. macrourus **8**: 12
Atilax paludinosus **1**: 98
aurochs **6**: 63
Australia, mammals introduced into **2**: 80; **5**: (97); **8**: 72
Avahi
  A. laniger **4**: 96
  A. occidentalis **4**: 96
Axis
  A. axis **6**: 10
  A. porcinus **6**: 10
aye-aye 4: 96, 97, <u>102–103</u>

B

babirusa 5: 74, 75, <u>86–87</u>
baboon 4: *8*, 40, 42, 42–43
  Chacma **4**: <u>56–57</u>
  gelada 4: 40, 42, 43, <u>62–63</u>
  hamadryas 4: 40, 43, <u>58–59</u>
  long-tailed *see* mangabey
  olive **4**: *10–11*
  sacred (hamadryas) **4**: 40, 43, <u>58–59</u>
  savanna 4: 40, 42–43, <u>54–57</u>
  yellow (savanna) **4**: 40, 42–43, <u>54–57</u>
Babyrousa babyrussa **5**: 74, <u>86–87</u>
badger 1: 34
  American 1: 32, <u>76–77</u>; **2**: (60)
  European 1: 32, 34, *35*, <u>78–81</u>
  hog **1**: 32
  honey 1: 32, <u>82–83</u>
  Indian ferret **1**: 32
  Palawan stink **1**: 32
Balaena mysticetus **3**: 55, <u>110–111</u>
Balaenoptera
  B. acutorostrata **3**: 55, <u>106–107</u>

  B. bonaerensis **3**: 107
  B. musculus **3**: 55, <u>98–101</u>
bamboo **2**: 98–99, 100; **4**: 97
bandicoot 10: (10), 24, 25,27
  eastern barred **10**: <u>8–9</u>
  giant **10**: 27
  golden **10**: 27
  large short-nosed (northern) **10**: <u>46–47</u>
  long-nosed **10**: 27
  mouse **10**: 27
  northern 10: <u>46–47</u>
  northern brown (northern) **10**: 27, <u>46–47</u>
  pig-footed **10**: 27
  rabbit-eared *see* bilby
  Raffray's **10**: 27
  rufous spiny **10**: 27
  Seram Island **10**: 27
  striped **10**: 27
  western barred **10**: 27
banteng **6**: 62
bark stripping **8**: 24
barnacles **3**: *57*, 92, 102, 108
Bassaricyon
  B. alleni **1**: 20
  B. gabbii **1**: 20
Bassariscus
  B. astutus **1**: 20
  B. sumichrasti **1**: 20
bat 1: *8*, *10*, 14; **7**: *12*, (37); **9**: <u>80–87</u>
  African slit-faced **9**: 82, 84
  American false vampire **9**: 86
  American little brown **9**: 87
  American pallid **9**: 84
  bat families **9**: 86–87
  Bechstein's **9**: <u>80–81</u>
  Brazilian (Mexican) free-tailed **9**: 82, (83), 84–85, *86*, <u>100–103</u>
  bulldog (fisherman) **9**: 87, <u>108–109</u>
  Daubenton's **9**: 87
  diadem roundleaf **9**: *86*
  disk-winged **9**: 87
  Egyptian fruit **9**: 86
  Egyptian rousette 9: <u>92–93</u>
  false vampire 9: 82, <u>98–99</u>
  fisherman 9: <u>108–109</u>
  free-tailed **9**: 87
  fruit **9**: 58, 80, 81, 86
  funnel-eared **9**: 87, *87*
  greater false vampire (false vampire) **9**: 82, <u>98–99</u>
  greater horseshoe **9**: 86
  guano (Mexican free-tailed) **9**: 82, (83), 84–85, *86*, <u>100–103</u>
  hairy big-eyed **9**: 85
  hairy-legged vampire **9**: 94
  hammerheaded **9**: 80, 86
  horseshoe **9**: 80, 87
  house (Mexican free-tailed) **9**: 82, (83), 84–85, *86*, <u>100–103</u>
  Indian greater false vampire (false vampire) **9**: 82, <u>98–99</u>
  Kitti's hog-nosed **1**: *11*, (11); **9**: 38, 80, 86
  lesser bulldog **9**: 108
  lesser horseshoe 9: <u>106–107</u>
  lesser long-nosed **9**: *84–85*
  little brown 9: 83, <u>104–105</u>
  long-eared 9: <u>110–111</u>
  long-tongued **9**: 86
  Mexican free-tailed 9: 82, (83), 84–85, *86*, <u>100–103</u>

  mouse-tailed **9**: 86
  mustached **9**: *87*
  New World leaf-nosed **9**: 87
  New Zealand short-tailed **9**: 86–87
  Old World false vampire **9**: 82, 87
  Old World leaf-nosed **9**: 87
  Old World sucker-footed **9**: 87
  rousette **9**: 86
  sheath-tailed **9**: 87
  slit-faced **9**: 87
  spear-nosed **9**: 84, *87*
  spectacled **9**: 87
  thumbless **9**: 87
  vampire 9: 84, (85), <u>94–97</u>
  whispering (long-eared) **9**: <u>110–111</u>
  white-winged vampire **9**: 94
  see also flying fox; pipistrelle
Bathyergidae **7**: *12*; **8**: 9
Bathyergus
  B. janetta **8**: 56
  B. suillus **8**: 56
Bdeogale
  B. crassicauda **1**: 98
  B. jacksoni **1**: 98
bear 2: 9; **5**: 9
  American black 2: 82, <u>90–93</u>
  Andean **2**: 82, *83*
  Asian black **2**: 82, *83*
  bear family 2: <u>82–83</u>
  big brown (brown) **2**: 82, *83*, 92, <u>94–97</u>
  brown 2: 82, *83*, 92, <u>94–97</u>
  dancing **2**: (97)
  "dawn bear" **2**: 82
  grizzly 2: 82, *83*, 92, <u>94–97</u>
  koala *see* koala
  Malaysian sun **2**: 82
  native Australian *see* koala
  panda *see* panda, giant
  polar 2: 9, 82, <u>84–89</u>; **3**: 83
  skunk *see* wolverine
  sloth **2**: 82, *83*
  spectacled **2**: 82, *83*
  sun **2**: 82, *83*
Beatragus hunteri **6**: 62
beaver 7: 8, 9, *10*, 11, *12*, 13; **8**: 29
  American 7: 28, 29, <u>30–33</u>
  beaver family 7: <u>28–29</u>
  Canadian (American) **7**: 28, 29, <u>30–33</u>
  Eurasian **7**: 28, 29
  mountain **7**: *12*, 14, 28, (29)
  mountain beaver family 7: <u>28–29</u>
  swamp *see* coypu
beetles, dung **2**: 76–77
beira **6**: 62
beluga 3: 55, <u>80–83</u>
bettong
  burrowing **10**: 48, *51*
  Tasmanian **10**: *8*
Bettongia lesueur **10**: 48
bilby 10: <u>44–45</u>
  greater **10**: 27, 44, *45*
  lesser **10**: 27, 44
binturong **1**: 88, *89*, 90, 91
biomedical research *see* medical research
bipedalism **4**: 10
bison
  American 6: 60, 62, <u>64–69</u>
  European **6**: 62, (66), 67
  wood **6**: 68
Bison
  B. bison **6**: 62, <u>64–69</u>
  B. bison athabascae **6**: 68
  B. bonasus **6**: 62, 66
blackbuck **6**: *61*, 62
Blarina brevicauda **9**: 28, <u>30–33</u>
Blastocerus dichotomus **6**: 10

Picture Credits

Abbreviations

NHPA   Natural History Photographic Agency

NPL   naturepl.com

OSF   Oxford Scientific Films

t = top; b = bottom; c = center; l = left; r = right

Jacket

tl caracal, Pete Oxford/naturepl.com; tr group of dolphins, Robert Harding Picture Library; bl lowland gorilla, Martin Rügner/Naturphotographie; br Rothchild's giraffe, Gerard Lacz/FLPA

8–9 Norbert Rosing/OSF; **11** Pete Oxford/NPL; **12** Roger Wood/Corbis; **13** Mark & Victoria Deeble/OSF; **14–15** Jonathan Scott; **15** David Tipling/OSF; **16** Frank Schneidermeyer/OSF; **17** Purdy & Matthews/Survival Anglia/OSF; **18–19** Kevin Schafer/NHPA; **20–21** Daniel J. Cox/OSF; **21** Mike Hill/OSF; **22** Alan & Sandy Carey/OSF; **23** Daniel J. Cox/OSF; **24–25** Frank Schneidermeyer/OSF; **26–27** Mike Hill/OSF; **27** John Downer/OSF; **28**t A. & M. Shah/Animals Animals/OSF; **28**b David W. Breed/OSF; **28–29** Anthony Bannister/ABPL/OSF; **30–31** Michael Fogden/OSF; **31** John Chellman/Animals Animals/OSF; **32** Stan Osolinski/OSF; **33** Norbert Rosing/OSF; **34–35** Gerard Lacz/NHPA; **36–37** Ken Cole/Animals Animals/OSF; **37** Nick Gordon/OSF; **38–39** Judd Cooney/OSF; **40–41** Konrad Wothe/OSF; **42–43** Daniel J. Cox/OSF; **44–45** Michael Sewell/OSF; **46–47** Martyn F. Chillmaid/OSF; **48–49** Konrad Wothe/OSF; **51** Glen & Rebecca Grambo; **52** Charlie Hamilton-James/NPL; **54–55** Alan & Sandy Carey/OSF; **55** Corbis; **56** Daniel J. Cox/OSF; **56–57** Konrad Wothe/OSF; **58–59** Victoria McCormick/Animals Animals/OSF; **59** T. Kitchen & V. Hurst/NHPA; **60–61** Richard Day/OSF; **62–63** Stan Osolinski/OSF; **63** Richard Packwood/OSF; **64–65** Eric Dragesco/Ardea; **66** Mark Hamblin/OSF; **67** Alan & Sandy Carey/OSF; **68–69** Erwin & Peggy Bauer/Bruce Coleman Collection; **70–71** Norbert Rosing/OSF; **72**t, **72**b Owen Newman/OSF; **73** Konrad Wothe/OSF; **74–75** Eyal Bartov/OSF; **76–77** Mark Deeble & Victoria Stone/OSF; **78–79** Adrian Bailey/OSF; **80–81** Simon King/NPL; **83**, **84–85** Daniel J. Cox/OSF; **86** Claude Steelman/Survival Anglia/OSF; **87** Jon A. Green/Animals Animals/OSF; **88–89** Norbert Rosing/OSF; **90–91**, **91** Daniel J. Cox/OSF; **92** Lynda Richardson/Corbis; **92–93** Wendy Shattil & Bob Rozinski/OSF; **93**, **94–95**, **96–97** Daniel J. Cox/OSF; **97** Djuro Huber/OSF; **98–99**, **100**, **101** Keren Su/OSF; **102–103** Clem Haagner/Ardea; **103** Terry Whittaker/Frank Lane Picture Agency; **104–105** Anup Shah/NPL; **105** Mark Deeble & Victoria Stone/OSF; **106–107** Peter Steyn/Ardea; **107** Terry Whittaker/Frank Lane Picture Agency; **108–109** Rafi Ben-Shahar/OSF; **110–111** Alan Root/Survival Anglia/OSF

Artists

Denys Ovenden, Priscilla Barrett with Michael Long, Graham Allen, Malcolm McGregor

While every effort has been made to trace the copyright holders of illustrations reproduced in this book, the publishers will be pleased to rectify any omissions or inaccuracies.